Gifford's
Gourmet De-Lites

Chef
Howard Gifford

Copyright 1988 by
Vitality House International, Inc.
1675 North Freedom Blvd. #11-C
Provo, Utah 84604

Telephone: 801-373-5100
To Order: Call Toll Free 1-800-637-0708

First Printing, December 1988
Second Printing, June 1989

This cookbook is a collection of recipes which have been gathered from various sources. Recipes have been adapted to meet a no-sugar, low-fat, high complex carbohydrate criteria.

Library of Congress Catalog Card Number: 88-51923

ISBN 0-912547-07-3

Printed in the United States of America

Front cover: Breast of Chicken Florentine with Marinara Sauce, p. 220; Wild Rice Pilaf, p. 221; Three-Bean Salad on Red Leaf Lettuce with Italian Dressing, p. 222; Baked Yellow Squash with Nutmeg, p. 222; Glazed Julienne Carrots, p. 223; Desperado Dessert, p. 224.

Dedication

A new horizon lay overhead, for the road I traveled warned "dead end." I knew the choice was mine--to finally hear, I needed but to listen. I knew, too, that with a strong desire and a daily commitment, I could overcome my addictions. From deep within my heart a light came shining through. Today the dream is alive, and with all my love I dedicate this book to you, my beautiful beloved daughter, Starr.

About the Author

Howard Gifford has been a professional chef for the past 12 years. He previously spent many years cooking in hotels and restaurants gaining vast experience in gourmet cooking. He began specializing in low-fat cooking in 1980 while working in health resorts. He not only prepared the meals at the resort, but taught classes on preparing easy healthy gourmet meals at home. He is a master at developing delicious recipes that are conducive to good health. In 1986, he owned Gifford's Gourmet De-Lite Cooking School. He ran an 8-week program teaching the techniques of low-fat, sugar, and sodium cooking. He is currently president of Gif's Gourmet De-Lites which features delicious menu's of the month and health food products. He works as a dietary supervisor of special diets with the Utah Alcoholism Foundation.

Table of Contents

Acknowledgements

I wish to thank the following individuals for their help and support:

To Dr. Edward Parent, Dr. Dennis Remington and Dr. Garth Fisher for giving me the opportunity to print my menu plan ideas. A special thanks to Dr. Edward Parent for all of his sound advice, support and patience.

To Mr. Alan Coombs and the staff at Green Valley Health Resort for all of their hard work, care, support and professionalism that they have given to all of their guests and others at their resort.

To K.J. Smith and Mitch Stowell for all of the long hours and hard work, of which there was plenty, that you gave to make this all happen.

To Barbara Higa for her editing skills and for the computer breakdown of all of the menus.

To Kathy Frandsen for editing and making sense of my writing.

To Borge B. Andersen and Associates, Inc. for their masterful photography.

To Janet Schaap, food stylist, for her beautiful arrangements on the photos.

To Fred Harrison and Design Workshop for art direction and layout on the cover.

To Rick Holmes and Rick Thayne for their graphics expertise.

And a special thanks to Doug Dinsmore and the staff at Brightway in St. George.

Introduction

For as long as I can remember, I have loved to cook. As I ground wheat at my grandparents' home, my childhood daydreams were of owning a neighborhood cafe like the one where all us kids hung out. That was probably the beginning of my culinary profession!

I have my choice of a profession, because it has been rich in satisfaction and rewards. But none of the years I have spent in the many phases of the food service industry have been as rewarding as these past few years, when I have specialized in preparing and teaching others to prepare low-fat, low-sugar, low-sodium recipes. I've spent much of the past few years working as executive chef for health resorts; guests have come from all over the world in a quest for weight control and better health.

At first, the health resort philosophy was standard and simple: guests spent all day exercising, and ate a diet restricted in calories and high in complex carbohydrates. Obviously, guests who restricted their food intake to less than 900 calories a day and who exercised almost all day experienced gratifying temporary weight loss. But the regimen at health resorts was an unrealistic lifestyle for long-term weight control. There was another problem, too--during the past few years, scientific research has shown how dangerous calorie-restricted dieting is.

The answer? "Sim-pli-fy, -fied, -ing: to make simple or easier." I first read *How to Lower Your Fat Thermostat* by Dennis Remington (M.D.), Garth Fisher (Ph.D.), and Edward Parent (Ph.D.) in late 1983. I was intrigued by what they had to say. In the years that followed, I became very convinced of the setpoint theory. So it was a great pleasure for me to become personally associated with the doctors in early 1987 at the Green Valley Health Resort, which featured their program. The results we were achieving there were most rewarding.

When they asked me to share some of my recipes in the form of a cookbook, I immediately imagined a menu-recipe format. Many people had been asking for a plan they could incorporate into their daily lifestyles--a plan that would be successful, but not too time-consuming.

In testing and retesting the information in this book, my goal was to keep it as simple as possible while preserving the elements required for successful weight control. In the pages that follow, I'm confident you'll find the helps you need to realize your goals and achieve permanent, healthy weight control!

Using the Menu Plan

The format of this book is a complete fourteen-day menu plan, emphasizing weight control and good health--and it's important to your success that you understand the elements involved. The sections that follow will show you how to get started, organize, shop, and prepare the menus included.

The Fourteen Days

In the chapters that follow you'll find fourteen days' worth of well-balanced and filling meals. These particular menus were chosen because they've worked over the years for people who were trying to lose weight and reestablish good health. Each day features three menus: one for breakfast, one for lunch, and one for dinner. This fourteen-day selection totals forty-two menus. What does that mean to you? If you prepare all forty-two menus, you'll repeat each entree only twice in a given month. You'll also enjoy a wide selection of menus, allowing you to choose menus that fit your lifestyle and your personal tastes.

The recipes and their variations create hundreds of menu combination possibilities--so use your imagination! With each day's menu you'll find a shopping list for perishable items; a master shopping list specifies the spices, extracts, frozen foods, and other nonperishables you'll need. A menu criteria sheet accompanying each day's menus lists helpful hints for organizing and preparing the meals.

The Menus

The fourteen breakfast menus, fourteen lunch menus, and fourteen dinner menus are designed to be as eye-appealing as possible. Why? Because we also eat with our eyes!

The breakfast menus are the easiest of the three meals. Recipe selections feature plenty of grains and cereals for a good balance of fiber.

The lunch menus are much easier than they appear: many of the soups, salads, and sandwiches featured can be prepared in advance. You'll love these time-savers--and if you work where there's a refrigerator and a microwave, you can enjoy a delicious alternative to fast-food meals!

The full-course dinner menus will demand the most attention. But don't feel over-whelmed--after you've prepared a few menus, you'll see that there's a real pattern and technique. Many of the menus call for another menu's leftover or a variation of another recipe. For example, the leftover "Blackberry Compote" from Day 1's breakfast is chilled and used as a preserve for that day's lunch. More information on the menus can be found in the Helpful Hints Section and the Planning Ahead Section.

The Recipes

A fourteen-day plan consisting of forty-two menus requires a lot of recipes. Realizing this, I've tried to pack the recipes with flavor while keeping ingredients to a minimum. As a result, you'll find that these recipes use plenty of spices, ex-tracts, juice concentrates, and other natural seasonings.

Recipes in this book are low in fat, oil, sugar, and salt. Simply stated, I've removed ingredients that are high in fat, sugar, and oil, and replaced them whenever pos-sible with a substitute. For example, imagine that a recipe calls for a heavy cream. Most heavy creams are 96 percent fat. By omitting the heavy cream and substitut-ing a mixture of skim milk and non-fat milk powder, you achieve a similar texture with virtually no fat.

Refined sugars and artificial sweeteners are replaced with unsweetened juice concentrates and natural flavors from fruits. Using juice concentrates as sweeteners soon enables you to really taste the foods you are preparing--they're no longer over-powered with sugars and artificial sweeteners! When using juice concentrates in dressings and desserts, allow time for the food to chill before serving; this enables the mixture to set up.

Included at the bottom of every recipe is a calculation based on a scoring system featured in *How to Lower Your Fat Thermostat*. **RCU** stands for Refined Carbohydrate Units. 1 RCU = 6 grams of sugar or honey; or 12 grams of white flour; or 24 grams of raisins or dates. According to Fat Thermostat guidelines you are allowed 2 RCU's per day. **FU** stands for Fat Unit. 1 FU = 6 grams of refined fat such as oil or mar-garine; or 8 grams of naturally occurring fat such as meat, milk, or eggs. You are allowed 4 FU's per day if you weigh less than 140 pounds and 5 FUs per day if you weigh more than 140 pounds. For further information, you will want to refer to the Table of Food Composition p. 187 - 208 in *How to Lower Your Fat Thermostat*.

Cal represents the number of calories in each serving, and **%Fat** represents the percentage of the total calories in that recipe derived from fat sources. **P, F,** and **C** represent the grams of protein, fat, and carbohydrate respectively for each serving of the recipe. **Na** represents the number of milligrams of sodium in each serving. **T** indicates that there is only a trace (less than 1 gram) of a nutrient.

With the foods featured here being low in fats and sugars, you can enjoy delicious entrees like lasagna, enchiladas, barbecued chicken, and burgers. Remember: you're eating foods that will satisfy your setpoint and help you maintain your health, not "dieting!"

The Menu Criteria Sheets

Have you ever started a recipe only to realize midway through that you're missing an ingredient? Or that it has to chill overnight? The menu criteria sheets included here will prevent those problems!

Each criteria sheet lists all the ingredients needed for the menu's recipes, listed in the order they appear in the recipe. You'll know ahead of time what you'll need for that menu--and you'll be able to spot anything you're missing before you go shopping. For ease of preparation, read the criteria sheet and gather all the ingredients you'll need for each recipe. Try putting all the ingredients together on a tray so you can find them easily; then put them all away at the same time when you're through.

You'll also find helpful menu hints and reminders on each criteria sheet. The "Food for Thought" section on each sheet will give you some welcome support.

The Master Shopping List

Most recipes call for only one teaspoon of a spice or extract--but when you scan the grocery store shelves, you'll find out you must purchase a full can or tin. And what happens when you invest in a tin of spices? Too often, you use a teaspoon or two--and then relegate it to the cupboard shelf, never to be used again.

That won't happen with the recipes in this book! Most of the ingredients these recipes require are ingredients you'll use over and over. All of the nonperishable items required in these recipes are listed on the master shopping list, and are divided into six categories: (1) spices and seasonings; (2) extracts; (3) flour, powders, and starch; (4) cereals, grains, and legumes; (5) frozen items; and (6) miscellaneous groceries. Each list contains the total amount of ingredients called for in the book. For example, onion powder is a frequent ingredient, so you'll need twenty-seven tablespoons of onion powder. Next to the amount called for will be the size and amount you should purchase. More ideas on using the master shopping list are found under "Shopping For a Menu."

Planning Ahead

As I give professional instruction to clients, I can never stress enough the importance of planning ahead. The following ideas and suggestions will help things run smoothly in the kitchen.

(1) Organize the Kitchen

Have you ever had to rummage through a cupboard or drawer for a pot or pan, or been unable to find a needed bowl, baking dish, or utensil? Start now by taking inventory of what you have. Keep what you'll need, and get rid of the rest. . .or at least store it out of the way!

Now get organized. Designate a specific area for everything you'll use in recipe preparation--food and non-food items alike. For example, you could organize spices in one area, extracts in another, and spoons and ladles in another. Remember that the recipes are low in fat, so use teflon and other nonstick equipment.

You might want to invest in a good set of cutlery if you don't have one--and remember to keep your knives sharp! (A sharp edge is far safer than a dull one.) Buy a good sharpener, and ask the salesman how to use it.

(2) Make the Kitchen Comfortable

It's important to be comfortable while in the kitchen--so eliminate things that make you uneasy while you're cooking, such as poor lighting, too many people in the kitchen, too much clutter, and too much walking back and forth locating equipment and ingredients. Frustration is due not to lack of skill, but to lack of organization. You might try playing music while you cook--it can help relax you, and it's fun to do the two-step while chopping onions!

(3) Create a Menu Board

Invest in a menu board; it can be something as simple as a chalk board. Write down the next menu you'll be preparing. You'll get an early start, and it helps remind you of an ingredient you need or a recipe that needs advanced preparation. It can also help you memorize menus and recipes the second time around. Best of all, it gives you something to look forward to!

(4) Visualize the Finished Product

Before you begin a menu, picture it in your mind: "see" how it's going to turn out, how the food will be served, how the table will be set, what kind of garnish you'll use, and so on. This kind of visualization will help build your confidence and will help in timing the meal. Take notes for awhile--jot down for future reference any problems you had in fixing a certain menu.

(5) Advance Preparation

Whenever you prepare a menu, look ahead to see if there is any advance menu preparation you can do with the same ingredients. For example, Day 2's dinner features a recipe for spaghetti sauce; the same recipe is used in Day 4's lunch. Since the sauce stores well, double the recipe when you're preparing it on Day 2. Simply refrigerate half until you need it for lunch on Day 4.

As another example, Day 4's breakfast menu calls for a Denver Omelet with onions, bell peppers, and turkey ham. Day 4's lunch menu features a pita pizza that calls for the same ingredients, so while you're fixing breakfast, dice some extra onions, peppers, and turkey ham for lunch.

Day 1's lunch menu features blueberry muffins--as does Day 3's breakfast menu. Double the batch while you're fixing them on Day 1, then simply refrigerate or freeze the extra muffins until Day 3.

These are just a few examples of how you can plan ahead on your menus. Do as much advanced preparation as you can--you'll save both time and energy!

Helpful Hints

To begin with, let's look at some basic cooking terms used in the menus. If you don't understand a term you find in a recipe, make sure you refer back to this section.

Cooking Terms

Bake: To cook food in an oven or oven-like appliance. Always bake a dish uncovered unless otherwise specified in the recipe.

Beat: To use a brisk up-and-over motion to make food smooth. You can use an electric mixer to achieve similar results.

Blend well: To use an electric blender to mix, chop, or puree food until it's smooth. You can also use a stirring motion by hand to give ingredients a uniform texture.

Boil: To cook in a liquid that is heated until bubbles rise to the surface of the mixture and break. In a full rolling boil, bubbles form rapidly throughout the mixture.

Chill: To refrigerate a mixture to reduce the temperature of the food, and to allow mixtures such as dressings and desserts to set and thicken before serving.

Chop: To chop foods into irregular-shaped pieces with a blender, food chopper, or a chef's knife. Chop foods when their shape is not important, as in potato salad, garden salads, and stuffings.

Cool: To allow a mixture to stand at room temperature to reduce the temperature of a food. To "cool quickly," refrigerate the mixture or set the container into a bowl of ice water.

Cube: To cut food into pieces that are the same size on all sides (at least 1/2 inch in diameter).

Dice: To cut food into cubes that are 1/8 to 1/4 inch on each side. Use a chef's knife.

Fold: To gently combine two or more ingredients.

Garnish: To decorate a food, usually with another food, for eye appeal.

Grate: To rub food across a grater to break it into fine particles.

Grind: To use a food grinder to cut food into very fine pieces; you can grind turkey or chicken and use it in burgers, meatloaf, sauces, or sausage.

Julienne: To slice food item lengthwise in 2 to 3 inch portions.

Mince: To cut foods into very tiny, shaped pieces. Use a utility knife for mincing.

Mix: To combine ingredients by stirring.

Puree: To convert a food into a liquid or paste with a blender or food processor.

Reduce: To thicken a mixture by boiling it rapidly and evaporating the liquid.

Saute: To cook food in a small amount of oil or liquid until tender.

Shred: To rub food on a shredder to form long, narrow pieces (commonly shredded foods include cabbage, vegetables, and cheese).

Simmer: To cook a mixture just below the boiling point. Bubbles burst before reaching the surface. "To simmer" does not mean to cook at the lowest possible temperature.

Stir: To use a spoon in a circular or figure-eight motion to combine ingredients.

Toss: To mix ingredients by lightly lifting and dropping with a fork or spoon.

Whisk: To blend a mixture by using a brisk up-and-over motion as
                rapidly as possible. Use a wire whip or a rotary beater operated
                by a hand crank.

Whip: To beat lightly and rapidly into a mixture; whipping makes food
                light and increases its volume.

Storing Foods

Store any perishable foods in the refrigerator or freezer as soon as possible after
you buy them. Don't let perishables stay at room temperature longer than two
hours--within two hours, microorganisms start growing on some foods. Keep the
temperature in your refrigerator between 34°F (1°C) and 40°F (4°C). Foods spoil
rapidly at temperatures higher than 40°F, and can alternately freeze and thaw at
temperatures lower than 34°F.

Refrigerate or freeze cooked foods or leftovers immediately after serving.
Remember: microorganisms start growing within two hours. Wrap all foods well
if you will be storing them after preparation, and use only containers with airtight
lids. Only keep foods that you'll use within a few days in the refrigerator.

The freezer is for long-term storage. The low temperature slows the growth of,
but does not kill, microorganisms. Use food stored in the freezer within sixty days
to insure quality and safety. Keep your freezer at 0°F (-18°C) or lower for maximum
protection. Thaw all frozen foods with care, and always thaw frozen foods in the
refrigerator. Remove frozen food items for a menu the day before so they will thaw
completely in the refrigerator. In an emergency, you can thaw frozen food in a
sealed bag under cold running water.

Nonperishable foods that are fairly sturdy--such as flours, grains, legumes,
potatoes, and onions--should be stored on a shelf at a temperature between 50°F
(10°C) and 70°F (21°C). Keep foods dry, well ventilated, and protected from sunlight.

Spices can be stored many ways. You might want to keep the spices you use most
often on the countertop nearest your preparation area. Spices can also be stored on
a cupboard shelf as long as there is good ventilation, no sunlight, and a temperature between 50°F and 70°F. Spices you don't use often can be stored in the
refrigerator as long as lids are sealed tightly. Spices have a shelf life of up to two

years; beyond two years they are usable, but lose some potency and flavor. To add life to your spice, occasionally shake the spice container gently to mix it.

Care in the kitchen begins with the proper use of your utensils and appliances. Follow manufacturer's instructions on cleaning and proper maintenance of your utensils and appliances. Anything that will contact the food--including hands, utensils, and countertops--must be kept clean. Always immediately scrub cutting boards, countertops, knives, and dishes after they are used to prepare raw meats or poultry; never use the same items for other food preparation until they have been scrubbed.

Food safety begins while shopping (for more information on shopping, see the section, "Shopping For a Menu Plan"). Always wash fruits and vegetables before preparing and serving them. Discard any wilted leaves on lettuce, spinach, or cabbage while rinsing. If you notice a foul odor or discoloration on meat or poultry, discard it. The more care you give, the better quality you will receive.

Basic Preparation Hints

Basic Dressing: This mixture of two parts cottage cheese to one part nonfat plain yogurt is featured in many menus. It is the base for most salad dressing, sandwich spreads, and a few desserts. I recommend that you make enough of the basic dressing to last for a couple of days. If mixture thickens or sets up, stir it gently until it's smooth.

Basic Creamer: You'll notice this basic creamer--a mixture of skim milk and nonfat milk powder--in many of the recipes. Use "natural" nonfat milk powder instead of "instant," which has a tendency to scald while cooking.

Basic Thickener: Many recipes call for cornstarch to be mixed with water. This is known as the basic thickener. If a recipe needs to be thickened more, simply add more of this mixture. Thickener will work best if you add it to a simmering or boiling mixture. Add the thickener slowly to the mixture, stirring until the mixture begins to thicken.

De-Lites Ketchup: Ketchup is called for often throughout the menus, so you should prepare enough ketchup for a few days. Stir or shake the ketchup before using.

Other recipes that can be prepared in bulk and frozen for future use:

Shopping For a Menu

Before explaining how to use the shopping lists that accompany the fourteen-day menu plan, let me discuss some shopping tactics that are especially useful for anyone.

Reading the Labels

Before you buy any food item, it's important to know exactly what you're buying. All food products have an ingredients list on the label, but you might not be familiar with many of the ingredients listed. As a rule of thumb, the fewer the unfamiliar ingredients, the more natural the product is likely to be. Most of the products you'll purchase for this menu plan are "pure and clean," so to speak, but you should still read each label to be sure.

Some product labels can be deceiving. For example, a product label may state that the product is 100 percent natural; when you read the label, though, you may find that the second ingredient listed is an artificial sweetener. Another brand of this same product may read "100 percent pure;" sure enough, the label lists no added ingredients.

Try to purchase products that have fat as 20 percent or less of the total per-serving calories. The book *How to Lower Your Fat Thermostat* gives a simple and comprehensive lesson on reading and figuring the percentage of fat in food products.

The Best Time to Shop

Most people shop as time permits--on the way home from work, on a day off, or on the weekend. Try the following to make your shopping easier:

1.   If you can, shop when the store is quiet and uncrowded; late evening or early morning is best.

2.   Know exactly what you're going to buy before you enter the store.

3.   Categorize your shopping list so you can get all the items needed from an area at one time.

4.   Choose a starting point and go through the aisles in sequence, with produce being last.

5.   Learn about the products you buy, such as meats, poultry, seafood, produce, and dairy. If you're unsure about any product, ask an employee for help.

6.   If you can, shop on the days the freshest products are available, such as produce and seafood.

7.   Give yourself ample time to properly put away and store the products you have purchased.

8.   Plan far enough ahead to avoid frequent trips to the grocery store.

9.   Buy products that store well in bulk when possible.

10.   When purchasing fresh foods, be picky. You want the best product available for your menus. Freshness begins at the grocery store.

Things to Avoid:

1.   Avoid shopping without a grocery list.

2.   Avoid shopping while hungry. This is where the saying, "we eat with our eyes" comes to life.

3.   If you can, avoid shopping at peak hours, such as rush hour, Friday afternoons, and Saturday afternoons.

4.   Avoid packages labeled "reduced for quick sale."

5.   Avoid bruised and wilted produce.

6.   Avoid purchasing canned goods that are dented or creased.

7.   If you can, avoid daily trips to the grocery store; they lead to unnecessary buying.

8.   Avoid products that are high in fats and sugars, such as ice cream, cookies, potato chips, and so on. If a food isn't on your list, you won't need it.

9.   Avoid the soft drinks aisle; some drinks have as many as 10 - 12 teaspoons of sugar per 12 oz. serving!

10. If you can, avoid shopping where quality assurance and customer service are not apparent.

Using the Shopping Lists

On the following pages you will find a master shopping list as well as a perishables shopping list for each day of the menu plan.

The master shopping list contains all nonperishable food products listed as ingredients in the recipes in this book. Each product specifies a total amount as well as the amount you should purchase. Some of the products may vary in size and in the way they are packaged, but you should readily find all or most of the products listed. Once you purchase the items specified on the master shopping list, all you need to complete your shopping is to purchase the items on the daily perishables lists. Some other shopping ideas for the fourteen-day plan include the following:

1.   If you're not using the master list, use the perishables shopping lists and your menu criteria sheet to list other items needed. The menu criteria sheet does not list quantities, but the items listed are used frequently.

2.   You can make your shopping list the traditional way--simply list the amount required in each recipe.

3.   Purchase frequently-used items in bulk, when available.

4.   Purchase items used frequently on the daily perishables shopping list all at one time. For example, many of the recipes call for eggs--in fact, there are about four dozen used in the fourteen days. Since eggs store well, buy two to four dozen at a time. Other frequently-used perishable items are cottage cheese, plain nonfat yogurt, skim milk, and whole wheat bread.

Master Shopping List

Spices

Item	Amount called for	Purchase
Allspice	2 teaspoon	1.25-ounce bottle
Anise, ground	1 teaspoon	1-ounce bottle
Bay leaves	2 leaves	0.12-ounce bottle
Basil, sweet	3 tablespoons	0.37-ounce bottle
Beef bouillon granules	15 tablespoons	5 1/2-ounce jar
Caraway, ground	1 teaspoon	1.75-ounce bottle
Cardamom, ground	1 teaspoon	1.75-ounce bottle
Celery seed, ground	4 teaspoons	1.62-ounce bottle
Chicken bouillon granules	27 tablespoons	(2) 5 1/2-ounce jars
Chili powder	3 1/2 teaspoons	2-ounce bottle
Cinnamon, ground	4 tablespoons	1.8-ounce bottle
Clove, ground	2 teaspoons	1.75-ounce bottle
Cumin, ground	3 teaspoons	1.5-ounce bottle
Dill weed	7 teaspoons	0.5-ounce bottle
Fennel, ground	4 teaspoons	1.5-ounce bottle
Fish bouillon granules	2 tablespoons	2-ounce bottle
Garlic powder	12 1/2 tablespoons	15-ounce bottle
Ginger	1/2 teaspoon	1.6-ounce bottle
Lemon peel (Schilling)	6 tablespoons	(2) 2-ounce bottles
Mace, ground	1/2 teaspoon	0.9-ounce bottle
Mint flakes	2 teaspoons	0.25-ounce bottle
Mustard, dry	7 teaspoons	1.75-ounce bottle
Nutmeg	2 teaspoons	1.8-ounce bottle
Onion powder	27 tablespoons	(4) 2.6-ounce bottles
Orange peel (Schilling)	4 teaspoons	1.5-ounce bottle
Oregano, ground	10 teaspoons	(2) 2-ounce bottle
Paprika	3 1/2 teaspoons	1.5-ounce bottle
Pepper, white	8 teaspoons	3.8-ounce can
Pepper, black	2 teaspoons	1.1-ounce bottle

Rosemary, ground	2 teaspoons	0.6-ounce bottle
Sage, rubbed	1 tablespoon	0.6-ounce bottle
Salt	7 teaspoons	9.25-ounce bottle
Tarragon leaves	2 teaspoons	0.37-ounce bottle
Thyme, ground	6 teaspoons	0.7-ounce bottle
Turmeric	1 1/2 teaspoons	0.37-ounce bottle

Extracts

Item	Amount called for	Purchase
Almond extract	3 teaspoons	1-ounce bottle
Banana extract	2 teaspoons	1-ounce bottle
Black walnut extract	1 teaspoon	1-ounce bottle
Butter flavor extract	1 1/4 teaspoons	1-ounce bottle
Cherry extract	5 1/2 teaspoons	(2) 1-ounce bottles
Coconut extract	1 teaspoon	1-ounce bottle
Maple extract	7 teaspoons	(2) 1-ounce bottles
Peppermint extract	1 teaspoon	1-ounce bottle
Vanilla extract	7 1/2 teaspoons	(2) 1/2-ounce bottles

Flour, Powders, Starch

Item	Amount called for	Purchase
Baking powder	11 tablespoons	(1) 10-ounce can
Baking soda	6 teaspoons	(1) 16-ounce box
Buttermilk powder (Saco)	36 tablespoons	(2) 5 1/2-ounce can
Yellow cornmeal	2 cups	(1) 20-ounce box
Cornstarch	103 tablespoons	(5) 16-ounce boxes
Nonfat milk powder (not instant)	10 cups	(1) 25 1/2-ounce box
Wheat germ	1/2 cup	(1) 10-ounce box
Whole wheat flour	22 cups	10 pounds

Cereals, Grains, Legumes

Item	Amount called for	Purchase
Bran, unprocessed	7 cups	(1) 16-ounce box
Cracked wheat	3 cups	(1) 20-ounce box
Whole wheat kernels	1 cup	(1) 16-ounce jar
Cream of wheat	1 cup	(1) 14-ounce box
Grapenuts cereal	14 cups	(2) 24-ounce boxes
Oatmeal	2 cups	(1) 13.8-ounce box
Brown rice	7 1/4 cups	(3) 2-pound bags
Whole wheat noodles	(2) 1-pound bags	(2) 1-pound bags
Whole wheat lasagna noodles	(1) 8-ounce box	(1) 8-ounce box
Dry split peas	(1) 1-pound bag	(1) 1-pound bag
Garbanzo beans	8 cups	(1) 4-pound bag
Fifteen-Bean Mix (Hamm's)	(1) 1-pound bag	(1) 1-pound bag

Frozen Foods

Item	Amount called for	Purchase
Apple juice concentrate	6 cups	(3) 16-ounce cans
Apple-raspberry concentrate	5 cups	(4) 12 ounce cans
Orange-banana-pineapple concentrate	11 tablespoons	(1) 12-ounce can
Orange juice concentrate	5 tablespoons	(1) 6-ounce can
Pineapple juice concentrate	1 1/2 cups	(1) 12-ounce can
Blackberries, unsweetened	6 1/2 cups	(4) 16-ounce bags
Blueberries, unsweetened	3 cups	(2) 16-ounce bags
Boysenberries, unsweetened	6 cups	(3) 16-ounce bags
Strawberries, unsweetened	1 1/2 cups	(1) 16-ounce bag
Sliced peaches, unsweetened	(1) 16-ounce bag	(1) 16-ounce bag
Raspberries, unsweetened	6 1/2 cups	(4) 16-ounce bags
Assorted melon balls	(2) 16-ounce bags	(2) 16-ounce bags
Brussels sprouts	(1) 16-ounce bag	(1) 16-ounce bag
Cut green beans	(1) 16-ounce bag	(1) 16-ounce bag

French-cut green beans	(1) 16-ounce bag	(1) 16-ounce bag
Peas	(1) 16-ounce bag	(1) 16-ounce bag

Miscellaneous Groceries

Item	Amount called for	Purchase
Dill juice	13 tablespoons	(1) 1-pint jar
Lime juice	3 tablespoons	(1) 6 1/2-ounce bottle
Lemon juice	10 tablespoons	(1) 8-ounce bottle
V-8 Juice	(1) 6-ounce can	(1) 6-ounce can
Tomato juice	2 cups	(2) 6-ounce cans
Apple cider vinegar	6 teaspoons	(1) 12-ounce bottle
Red wine vinegar	10 tablespoons	(1) 12-ounce bottle
White wine vinegar	6 tablespoons	(1) 12-ounce bottle
Tarragon vinegar	1/4 cup	(1) 12-ounce bottle
Apricot nectar	1/2 cup	(1) 5 1/2-ounce can
Cooking sherry	2 ounces	(1) 12-ounce bottle
Worchestershire sauce	20 tablespoons	(2) 12-ounce bottles
Soy sauce (Kikkoman's mild)	8 tablespoons	(1) 10-ounce bottle
Tabasco sauce	2 1/2 teaspoons	(1) 2-ounce bottle
Liquid smoke	2 1/2 teaspoons	(1) 4-ounce bottle
Kitchen Bouquet	1 tablespoon	(1) 4-ounce bottle
Tomato puree	24 cups	(8) 29 1/2-ounce cans
Tomato sauce	3 cups	(1) 29 1/2-ounce can
Crushed pineapple	2 cups	(2) 15-ounce cans
Chunk pineapple	(2) 15-ounce cans	(2) 15-ounce cans
Tuna, in water	(2) 6 1/2-ounce cans	(2) 6 1/2-ounce cans
Chopped clams	(4) 5 1/2-ounce cans	(4) 5 1/2-ounce cans
Three-bean salad	(1) 15 1/2-ounce can	(1) 15 1/2-ounce can
Pinto beans, canned	(1) 15 1/2-ounce can	(1) 15 1/2-ounce can
Pear halves, in juice	(1) 29 1/2-ounce can	(1) 29 1/2-ounce can
Applesauce, unsweetened	(1) 15 1/2-ounce can	(1) 15 1/2-ounce can
Prepared horseradish	1 teaspoon	(1) 2-ounce jar
Prepared mustard	5 teaspoon	(1) 8-ounce jar
Diced pimiento	5 1/2 tablespoons	(3) 2-ounce jars
Diced green chilies	5 1/2 tablespoons	(1) 7-ounce caan
Bamboo shoots, sliced	1 4 1/2-ounce can	(1) 4 1/2-ounce can

Miscellaneous Groceries (cont.)

Item	Amount called for	Purchase
Water chestnuts, sliced	1 4 1/2-ounce can	(1) 4 1/2-ounce can
Unflavored gelatin (Knox)	6 1/2 tablespoons	(1) 16-package box
Butter Buds	8 packets	1 box
Garlic bread sticks	8-ounce box	(1) 8-ounce box
Raisins	4 1/2 cups	(1) 2-pound bag
Oil	19 tablespoons	1 quart bottle
Nonstick vegetable spray	1 large can	(1) 32-ounce can

Perishables Shopping List

Day 1

Item	Amount day calls for	Purchase
Chicken breasts	8 ounces	8 ounces
Flank steak	1 pound	1 pound
Apples	8 medium	8 medium
Carrots	10 medium	10 medium
Celery	4 stalks	1 bundle
Lettuce	2 medium heads	2 medium heads
Mushrooms	6 medium	6 medium
Onions	8 small	8 small
Potatoes	4 medium	4 medium
Assorted fresh fruit (your choice)	See Criteria Sheet (breakfast)	your choice
Low fat cottage cheese	1 cup	1 pint
Eggs	6	1 dozen
Skim milk	5 cups	1/2 gallon
Plain nonfat yogurt	1/2 cup	1 pint
Whole wheat bread	8 slices	1 loaf

Day 2

Item	Amount day calls for	Purchase
Turkey ham	8 ounces	(1) 2-pound roll
Chicken breasts (boneless)	10 ounces	(2) 5-ounce breasts
Ground turkey	1 pound	1 pound

Day 2 (cont.)

Item	Amount day calls for	Purchase
Bell peppers	5 medium	5 medium
Carrots	2 medium	2 medium
Celery	2 stalks	2 stalks
Cucumbers	1 small	1 small
Lettuce	1 head	1 head
Mushrooms	12 large	12 large
Honeydew	1 medium	1 medium
Tomatoes	2 medium	2 medium
Low fat cottage cheese	2 cups	1 pint
Eggs	4 large	1 dozen
Plain nonfat yogurt	1/2 cup	1 pint
Skim milk	1 3/4 cups	1 pint
whole wheat bread	8 slices	1 loaf

Day 3

Item	Amount day calls for	Purchase
Chicken breasts (boneless)	10 ounces	(2) 5-ounce breasts
Turkey breast	6 ounces, cooked	8 ounces (deli)
Turkey ham	3 ounces	optional
Bean sprouts	3 ounces	3 ounces
Broccoli	1 cup	1 small bunch
Carrots (diced)	1 cup	1 pound
Cauliflower	1 cup	1 small head
Celery	5 stalks	1 bunch
Cucumber	1 medium	1 medium
Mushrooms (sliced)	1 cup	6 large
Onions, yellow	3 large	3 large
Onions, green	2 stalks	1 bunch
Bell peppers	3 medium	3 medium
Red peppers	1 medium	1 medium

Potatoes	1 medium	1 medium
Tomatoes	2 medium	2 medium
Apples, Red Delicious	1 large	1 large
Bananas	2 medium	1 bunch
Honeydew melon	1 small	1 small
Low fat Cottage cheese	1 cup	1 pint
Eggs	2 large	1 dozen
Skim milk	approx. 1 quart	1 quart
Plain nonfat yogurt	1 1/2 cups	1 pint
Whole wheat pita bread	4 slices	(1) 6-slice bag

Day 4

Item	Amount day calls for	Purchase
Ground turkey	1 pound	1 pound
Turkey ham	2 ounces	1 pound
Broccoli	1 bunch	1 bunch
Celery	2 stalks	1 small bunch
Head lettuce	1 head	1 head
Leaf lettuce	1 head	1 head
Mushrooms	1 pound	1 pound
Onions, yellow	2 medium	2 medium
Onions, green	1 stalk	1 bunch
Bell peppers	1 large	1 large
Potatoes	6 large	6 large
Tomatoes	2 medium	2 medium
Zucchini	1 medium	1 medium
Bananas	2 medium	2 medium
Cantaloupe	1 small	1 small
Eggs	4 large	1 dozen
Skim milk	1 1/2 cups	1 pint
Plain nonfat yogurt	1 cup	1 pint
Mozzarella cheese, part skim	6 ounces	8 ounces
Whole-grain bread	4 slices	1 loaf
Whole wheat pita bread	6 pita slices	(1) 6-slice bag

Day 5

Item	Amount day calls for	Purchase
Chicken breast tenders	18 ounces	18 ounces
Ground turkey	1/2 pound	1/2 pound
Turkey ham	2 ounces	1 pound
Assorted fresh vegetables	your choice	your choice
Head lettuce	1 head	1 head
Leaf lettuce, red	1 small head	1 small head
Mushrooms	optional	optional
Tomatoes	3 medium	3 medium
Apples	2 medium	2 medium
Fresh fruit (for garnish)	leftovers	use leftovers
Lite American cheese	2 ounces	(1) 8-slice pack
Low fat cottage cheese	8 ounces	1 pint
Eggs	6 large	1 dozen
Skim milk	2 cups	1 pint
Plain nonfat yogurt	1/4 cup	1 pint
Whole wheat bread	8 slices	1 loaf

Day 6

Item	Amount day calls for	Purchase
Red snapper fillets	1 pound	1 pound
Apple, red	1 medium	1 medium
Apple, green	1 medium	1 medium
Bananas	2 medium	2 medium
Grapes, seedless	1 cup	1 small bunch
Oranges	3 medium	3 medium
Celery	4 stalks	1 bunch
Cabbage, green	1 small head	1 small head
Lettuce, red leaf	4 leaves	1 small head
Mushrooms	approx. 1 pound	1 pound
Onions	2 1/2 large	3 large

Potatoes	2 medium	2 medium
Spinach	2 bunches	2 bunches
Zucchini	2 medium	2 medium
Low fat cottage cheese	1 cup	1 pint
Skim milk	2 cups	1 pint
Plain nonfat yogurt	1 1/2 cup	1 pint
Whole wheat bread	1 loaf	1 loaf

Day 7

Item	Amount day calls for	Purchase
Chicken breast tenders	8 ounces	8 ounces
Ground turkey	2 pounds	2 pounds
Celery	2 stalks	1 bunch
Head lettuce	1 large head	1 large head
Mushrooms	4 large	1/4 pound
Red onions	1 small	1 small
Potatoes	4 medium	4 medium
Tomatoes	5 large	5 large
Assorted fresh fruit	your choice	your choice
Honeydew melon	1 medium	1 medium
Lite American cheese	4 slices	(1) 8-slice pack
Low fat cottage cheese	1 cup	1 pint
Eggs	2 large	1 dozen
Skim milk	5 cups	1/2 gallon
Plain nonfat yogurt	1/2 cup	1 pint
Multi-grain buns	4	1 8-pack

Day 8

Item	Amount day calls for	Purchase
Chicken breasts	4	4
Turkey ham	4 ounces (optional)	1 pound

Day 8 (cont.)

Item	Amount day calls for	Purchase
Asparagus	desired amount	desired amount
Carrots	4 medium	4 medium
Celery	3 stalks	1 bunch
Cucumber	1 medium	1 medium
Lettuce, head	1 head	1 head
Lettuce, red leaf	8 leaves	1 head
Mushrooms	7 large	7 large
Onions, red	1 small	1 small
Onions, yellow	2 medium	2 medium
Potatoes	2 large	2 large
Peppers, red	1 medium	1 medium
Parsley	2 Tbs chopped	1 bunch
Scallions	2 Tbs chopped	2 scallions
Zucchini	1 small	1 small
Red apples	2 medium	2 medium
Bananas	1 medium	1 medium
Strawberries	1 pint	1 pint
Bleu cheese crumbles	1 teaspoon	1 small block
Low fat cottage cheese	trace	
Eggs	4 large	1 dozen
Mozzarella cheese, part skim	4 ounces	8-ounce pack
Skim milk	1 cup	1 pint
Plain nonfat yogurt	2 1/2 cups	2 pints

Day 9

Item	Amount day calls for	Purchase
Ground turkey	1 pound	1 pound
Broccoli	1 bunch	1 bunch
Lettuce, head	2 heads	2 heads
Lettuce, romaine	1 head	1 head

Lettuce, endive	1 head	1 head
Mushrooms	6 medium	6 medium
Onions	2 medium	2 medium
Bell peppers	2 medium	2 medium
Apple	1 small	1 small
Bananas	2 medium	2 medium
Cantaloupe	1 quarter	1 small
Grapes, seedless	1 cup	1 small bunch
Oranges	1 medium	1 medium
Assorted fresh fruit	your choice	your choice
Strawberries	1/2 pint	1 pint
Low fat cottage cheese	5 cups	3 pints
Eggs	2 large	1 dozen
Skim milk	2 1/4 cups	1 quart
Plain nonfat yogurt	1/2 cup	1 pint
Mozzarella cheese, part skim	1 pound	1 pound
Whole wheat English muffins	desired amount	(1) 6-muffin bag

Day 10

Item	Amount day calls for	Purchase
Chicken breast tenders	1 1/2 pounds	1 1/2 pounds
Turkey ham	4 ounces	1 pound
Carrots	3 medium	3 medium
Celery	3 stalks	1 bunch
Cucumber	1 medium	1 medium
Lettuce, head	1 small head	1 small head
Onions	4 small	4 small
Potatoes	4 medium	4 medium
Bell peppers	3 medium	3 medium
Tomatoes	2 medium	2 medium
Grapefruit	2 medium	2 medium
Strawberries	1 cup	1 pint
Lite American cheese	4 slices	(1) 8-slice pack
Mozzarella cheese, part skim	4 ounces	8 ounces
Eggs	1 large	1 dozen
Low fat cottage cheese	1 1/2 cups	1 pint

Day 10 (cont.)

Item	Amount day calls for	Purchase
Skim milk	1 cup	1 pint
Plain nonfat yogurt	1/2 cup	1 pint
Whole wheat flour tortillas	4	1 dozen

Day 11

Item	Amount day calls for	Purchase
Flank steak	1 pound	1 pound
Cooked crab	4 ounces	4 ounces
Cooked baby shrimp	4 ounces	4 ounces
Assorted fresh fruit	your choice	your choice
Lettuce, head	1 head	1 head
Mushrooms	10 medium	1 pound
Onion	1 mediu,	1 medium
Parsley	1 tablespoon	1 small bunch
Potatoes	4 medium	4 medium
Fresh spinach	1 cup torn leaves	1 bunch
Tomatoes	2 medium	2 medium
Assorted fresh fruit	your choice	your choice
Lemons	2 medium	2 medium
Strawberries	1 cup	1 pint
Mozzarella cheese, part skim	2 ounces	8 ounces
Low fat cottage cheese	1/2 cup	1 pint
Eggs	2 large	1 dozen
Skim milk	1 cup	1 pint
Plain nonfat yogurt	1 1/4 cup	1 pint
Whole-grain bread	4 to 8 slices	1 loaf

Day 12

Item	Amount day calls for	Purchase
Boneless chicken breasts	4 5-ounce breasts	(4) 5-ounce breasts
Ground turkey	1 1/2 pounds	2 pounds
Carrots	2 medium	2 medium
Celery	1/4 cup leaves	1 bunch
Fresh garlic	3 cloves	1 whole
Lettuce, head	1 cup shredded	1 small head
Red leaf lettuce	8 leaves	1 head
Onions	3 small	3 small
Fresh parsley	2 tablespoons	1 small bunch
Bell peppers	2 medium	2 medium
Yellow squash	(1) 5-pound piece	(1) 5-pound piece
Fresh squash	1 small bunch	1 small bunch
Tomatoes	2 medium	2 medium
Cantaloupe	1 small	1 small
Strawberries	2 cups	1 pint
Eggs	2 large	1 dozen
Skim milk	2 cups	1 pint
Plain nonfat yogurt	1 cup	1 pint
Mozzarella cheese, part skim	12 ounces	1 pound
Corn tortillas	4	1 dozen

Day 13

Item	Amount day calls for	Purchase
Cooked crab	1/4 pound	1/4 pound
Boneless chicken breasts	1 pound	1 pound
Cod fillets	1 pound	1 pound
Scallops	1/4 pound	1/4 pound
Cooked baby shrimp	1/4 pound	1/4 pound
Green cabbage	1 small head	1 small head
Carrots	2 medium	2 medium

Day 13 (cont.)

Item	Amount day calls for	Purchase
Celery	2 stalks	1 bunch
Mushrooms	1 pound	1 pound
Bell peppers	3 medium	3 medium
Red peppers	1 medium	1 medium
Onions	3 small	3 small
Potatoes	2 medium	2 medium
Fresh spinach	2 bunches	2 bunches
Tomato	1 medium	1 medium
Zucchini	1 medium	1 medium
Bananas	2 medium	2 medium
Lemons	2 small	2 small
Pineapple	1 whole	1 whole
Honeydew melon	1 medium	1 medium
Low fat cottage cheese	1/2 cup	1 pint
Eggs	2 large	1 dozen
Skim milk	2 cups	1 pint
Plain nonfat yogurt	2 cups	1 pint
Whole-grain bread	4 to 8 slices	1 loaf

Day 14

Item	Amount day calls or	Purchase
Chicken breasts	1 pound	1 pound
Chicken legs	1 pound	1 pound
Ground chicken	1 pound	1 pound
Carrots	3 medium	3 medium
Celery	3 stalks	1 bunch
Eggplant	1 small	1 small
Lettuce, head	1 small head	1 small head
Onions	3 medium	3 medium
Potatoes	12 medium	12 medium

Tomato	1 medium	1 medium
Apples	2 medium	2 medium
Bananas	2 medium	2 medium
Cantaloupe	1 small	1 small
Honeydew melon	1 small	1 small
Grapes, seedless	1 cup	1 small bunch
Oranges	2 medium	2 medium
Mozzarella cheese, part skim	6 ounces	8 ounces
Low fat cottage cheese	1 cup	1 pint
Eggs	6 large	1 dozen
Skim milk	2 cups	1 pint
Plain nonfat yogurt	2 cups	1 pint
Multi-grain buns	4	(1) 8-bun package

Gifford's

D A Y   1

BREAKFAST

De-Lites Fitness Granola

Assorted Fresh Fruit

Whole Wheat Toast with Blackberry Compote

LUNCH

PAGE 36

De-Licious Chicken Noodle Soup

*Fresh Chilled Iceberg Salad
with Assorted Fresh Vegetables*

De-Lite-ful Dill Dressing

Hot Blueberry Muffin with Fruit Preserve

DINNER

PAGE 42

Hearty Old-Fashioned Beef Stew

*Carrot and Pineapple Salad
Served Over Chilled Shredded Lettuce*

Baked Cornbread

Hot Apple Strudel Dessert

Breakfast Menu Criteria

Products You'll Need

Granola:

Cracked wheat cereal
Old-fashioned oats (raw)
Long-grain brown rice
Grapenuts cereal
Whole Wheat Bread
Almond extract
Banana extract
Coconut extract
Skim milk

Assorted Fresh Fruit:
(your choice)

Apples	Nectarines
Bananas	Oranges
Cantaloupe	Peaches
Crenshaw	Pears
Grapes	Pineapple
Grapefruit	Plums
Honeydew	

Compote:

Frozen blackberries (unsweetened)
Apple-raspberry juice concentrate (unsweetened)
Cornstarch

Helpful Menu Hints

1. This meal can be prepared more quickly if you cook the rice ahead of time.

2. While the cracked wheat is cooking, start the compote.

3. Cut the fruit, set the table, and start toasting the bread while completing step #2.

Food for Thought

It only takes a little effort to make your meal attractive with the use of clever garnishes, creative table settings, and so on. Remember: we eat with our eyes!

Breakfast Recipes

De-Lites Fitness Granola

4	C	water
1	C	cracked wheat cereal
1	C	old-fashioned oats (raw)
1	C	cooked long-grain brown rice
¼	C	Grapenuts cereal

dash of almond, banana, and coconut extracts

In a medium saucepan, bring water to a boil. Add cracked wheat; stir, and reduce heat to simmer. Cover and cook for 12 minutes, stirring occasionally. Remove from heat. Add remaining ingredients and mix well.
May be served with skim milk.

Yield: approximately 8 servings

	RCU	FU	Cal	%Fat	P	F	C	Na
per serving	0	0	158	8	4	1	24	87

Blackberry Compote

2	C	water
1	C	frozen blackberries (unsweetened)
¼	C	apple-raspberry juice concentrate (unsweetened)

In separate bowl mix:

3	T	cornstarch
½	C	water

In a medium saucepan, bring water and juice concentrate to a boil. Slowly stir in cornstarch mixture. Reduce heat, stirring constantly until mixture is thick. Add blackberries and mix well. Remove from heat.

Yield: 6 (1/2 cup) servings

	RCU	FU	Cal	%Fat	P	F	C	Na
per serving	0	0	50	3	T	T	12	3

Lunch Menu Criteria

Products You'll Need

Soup:

Chicken breast
Onion
Celery
Carrots
Skim milk
Nonfat milk powder
Whole wheat noodles
Cornstarch
Chicken boullion granules
Onion powder
Ground celery seed
Worchestershire sauce
White pepper
Ground cloves
Cardamom
Liquid smoke

Salad:

Iceberg lettuce
Assorted fresh vegetables

Dressing:

Low fat cottage cheese
Plain nonfat yogurt
Dill juice
Chicken boullion granules
Dill weed
Onion powder
Apple juice concentrate
    (unsweetened)
White pepper

Muffins:

Whole wheat flour
Unprocessed bran
Baking powder
Baking soda
Salt
Egg whites
Oil
Skim milk
Apple juice concentrate
    (unsweetened)
Frozen blueberries

Helpful Menu Hints

1.   Prepare lettuce ahead of time.

2.   Prepare muffins first; while they are baking, you'll have 25 minutes in which to prepare other items on the menu.

3.   For the assorted vegetables with your salad, use leftovers from the soup ingredients, such as carrots, celery, and onion.

Food for Thought

Practice makes perfect: remember, it gets easier!

Lunch Recipes

De-Licious Chicken Noodle Soup

8	oz.	boneless chicken breast (skinless), diced
1	C	onion, diced
1	C	celery, diced
1	C	carrot, diced
4	C	water

Mix together:

1	C	skim milk
½	C	nonfat milk powder

Mix together:

3	T	cornstarch
½	C	water
2	T	chicken bouillon granules
2	T	onion powder
½	tsp	ground celery seed
1	tsp	Worchestershire sauce

pinch of white pepper
pinch of ground clove
pinch of cardamom
a drop of liquid smoke

2	C	cooked whole wheat noodles, chopped in 1-inch pieces

Coat a 3-quart saucepan lightly with a nonstick spray. Saute chicken and vegetables together on medium-high heat until vegetables are tender. Add a small amount of water to the mixture to gather caramelizing from pan; add remaining water. Bring to a boil. Add all spices; blend well. Add cornstarch mixture slowly, stirring constantly until mixture starts to thicken. Reduce heat. Add milk mixture and stir until blended. Add noodles; simmer 10 minutes, stirring occasionally.

Yield: 1 1/2 quarts or 6 (1 cup) servings

	RCU	FU	Cal	%Fat	P	F	C	Na
per serving	0	0	186	8	15	2	27	107

Garden Salad

1 medium head iceberg lettuce
assorted fresh vegetables

Remove outer leaves of iceberg lettuce head. Discard any wilted or discolored outer leaves. Hit stem end sharply on tabletop to loosen core. Twist and remove core. Place lettuce head bottom side up, under cold water, and rinse well. Invert lettuce head and let water drain thoroughly. Place in plastic bag; refrigerate a few hours to crisp.

Tear lettuce leaves into pieces and place in salad bowl. (Chopping lettuce with a knife bruises the leaves.)

Combine lettuce leaves with assorted fresh vegetables of your choice.

Yield: approximately 4 servings

	RCU	FU	Cal	%Fat	P	F	C	Na
per serving	0	0	7	13	.6	T	1	5

Basic Dressing

1	C	low fat cottage cheese
½	C	plain nonfat yogurt

Combine cottage cheese and yogurt in blender, and blend together until smooth.

Note: This basic dressing is used in many of the recipes in this book.

Dill Dressing

1	C	Basic Dressing
2	T	dill juice
1	tsp	chicken bouillon granules
1	tsp	dill weed
1	tsp	onion powder
1	tsp	apple juice concentrate (unsweetened)

pinch of white pepper

In mixing bowl, gently whisk all ingredients until blended. Let stand a few minutes. Repeat. Chill before serving.

Yield: 5 (1/4 cup) servings

	RCU	FU	Cal	%Fat	P	F	C	Na
per serving	0	0	57	15	8	1	4	203

Hot Blueberry Muffins

1¼	C	whole wheat flour
¾	C	bran, unprocessed
1½	tsp	baking powder
½	tsp	baking soda
¼	tsp	salt
2		egg whites
2	tsp	oil
¾	C	skim milk
3	T	apple juice concentrate (unsweetened)
½	C	frozen blueberries (unsweetened)

Coat a nonstick muffin pan lightly with a nonstick spray. In small mixing bowl, beat egg with fork; beat in milk, juice concentrate, and oil. In large mixing bowl stir together the flour, bran, baking powder, soda, and salt. Make a well in the center of the flour mixture. Add the egg mixture all at once. Stir gently just until blended. Fold in blueberries. Spoon into the prepared muffin pan, filling each cup 2/3 full. Bake in 400° oven 20 to 25 minutes.

Yield: 12 muffins

	RCU	FU	Cal	%Fat	P	F	C	Na
per muffin	0	0	77	15	4	1	15	137

Dinner Menu Criteria

Products You'll Need

Stew:

Flank steak
Onions
Beef bouillon granules
Worchestershire sauce
Potatoes
Carrots
Celery
Onion powder
Garlic powder
Chili powder
Dry mustard
Ground thyme
Pepper
Mushrooms
Tomato puree
Peas

Salad:

Lettuce
Carrots
Raisins
Crushed pineapple
Chicken bouillon granules
Cinnamon
Nutmeg

Cornbread:

Yellow cornmeal
Whole wheat flour
Baking powder
Baking soda
Salt
Egg whites
Skim milk
Nonfat milk powder
Apple juice concentrate
Oil

Strudel:

Red delicious apples
Cornstarch
Cinnamon
Allspice
Anise seed
Cloves
Apple juice (unsweetened)
Butter flavor extract
Black walnut extract
Grapenuts cereal

Helpful Menu Hints

1. Start the stew first.

2. Prepare the strudel next, then the cornbread.

3. Leftover stew and cornbread freeze well for future use.

Food for Thought

Commitment, dedication, and desire harvest great rewards.

Dinner Recipes

Hearty Old-Fashioned Beef Stew

1	lb	beef flank steak, cut into 1-inch squares
6	sm	onions, quartered
2½	T	beef bouillon granules
2	T	Worchestershire sauce
2	C	water
4	med	potatoes, peeled and quartered
4		carrots, scrubbed and sliced
2	stalks	celery, cut into 1-inch squares
1½	T	onion powder
1	T	garlic powder
1	tsp	chili powder
1	tsp	dry mustard
½	tsp	ground thyme
¼	tsp	pepper
6	med	mushrooms, quartered
1	C	water
½	C	tomato puree
¼	C	garden peas

Coat a large saucepan lightly with a nonstick spray. Cook beef over medium heat until browned. Add onion and cook until onions become transparent. Add beef bouillon granules and Worchestershire sauce. Stir and allow mixture to caramelize. Add water quickly. Blend well. Add potatoes, carrots, and celery; simmer until potatoes are tender. Add remaining ingredients except peas. Blend well. Simmer an additional 15 minutes, stirring occasionally. Remove from heat. Add peas. Serve.

Yield: 8 servings

	RCU	FU	Cal	%Fat	P	F	C	Na
per serving	0	.5	185	19	16	4	23	123

Carrot and Pineapple Salad

Served Over Chilled Shredded Lettuce

2	C	shredded lettuce
4		carrots, shredded
½	C	raisins
½	C	Basic Dressing *(see recipe, Day 1, lunch)*
½	C	pineapple, crushed, drained (reserve liquid)
¼	tsp	chicken bouillon granules
¼	tsp	ground cinnamon

pinch of nutmeg

In salad bowl, gently toss carrots and raisins. In a separate mixing bowl, gently whisk remaining ingredients (except lettuce) together until blended. Fold this mixture into carrot mixture. Serve over shredded lettuce.

Yield: 6 to 8 servings

	RCU	FU	Cal	%Fat	P	F	C	Na
per serving	0	0	89	6	4	1	18	100

Baked Cornbread

2	C	yellow cornmeal
1	C	whole wheat flour
2	tsp	baking powder
½	tsp	baking soda
¼	tsp	salt
4		egg whites
1	C	skim milk
½	C	nonfat milk powder
¼	C	apple juice concentrate (unsweetened)
2	tsp	oil

In a large mixing bowl, sift together cornmeal, flour, baking powder, baking soda, and salt. Make a well in center of the mixture. In small bowl whisk gently together remaining ingredients. Pour this mixture into well. Stir gently until blended. Spray a 13x9x2 baking pan lightly with nonstick spray. Pour batter into pan. Bake in 375° oven for 30 minutes or until a wooden pick inserted in the center comes out clean.

Yield: 24 (2-inch) squares

	RCU	FU	Cal	%Fat	P	F	C	Na
per serving	0	0	77	11	3	1	14	94

Hot Apple Strudel Dessert

8		red delicious apples, peeled and cored
2	T	cornstarch
1	T	ground cinnamon
½	tsp	ground allspice
½	tsp	ground anise seed
¼	tsp	ground cloves
1½	C	apple juice (unsweetened)
1	tsp	butter flavor extract
1	drop	black walnut extract
2	C	Grapenuts cereal

Chop apples. In a mixing bowl, toss apples, cornstarch, and spices thoroughly. Pour in juice and extracts. Stir until blended. Lightly coat a 13x9x2 baking dish with a nonstick spray. Pour 1 cup Grapenuts cereal evenly into pan, reserving second cup. Pour apple mixture evenly over Grapenuts. Sprinkle remaining cup of Grapenuts evenly over apple mixture. Bake in 375° oven 30 minutes, or until apples are tender. Remove and serve.

Yield: 8 to 10 servings

	RCU	FU	Cal	%Fat	P	F	C	Na
per serving	0	0	164	3	3	.5	40	161

Gifford's

D A Y 2

BREAKFAST

*Whole Wheat Pancakes
with Raspberry Compote or Maple Syrup*

Assorted Fresh Fruit

Turkey Ham Slices

LUNCH

PAGE 54

Chicken Ala King Served with Toast Points

Wild Rice Pilaf

Steamed Garden Peas

Carrot and Celery Sticks

Quartered Honeydew Melon

DINNER

PAGE 56

Spaghetti with De-Licious Meat Sauce

Fresh Garden Salad with Italian Dressing

Steamed Green Beans

Garlic Bread Sticks

Godfather's Peppermint Pie

Breakfast Menu Criteria

Products You'll Need

Pancakes:

Whole wheat flour
Wheat germ
Baking powder
Baking soda
Salt
Eggs
Oil
Skim milk
Apple juice concentrate (unsweetened)
Vanilla

Compote:

Raspberries (unsweetened)
Apple-raspberry concentrate
(unsweetened)
Cornstarch

Syrup:

Apple juice concentrate
  (unsweetened)
Maple extract
Cornstarch

Assorted Fresh Fruit:
  (your choice)

Apples	Nectarine
Bananas	Orange
Cantaloupe	Peaches
Crenshaw	Pears
Grapes	Pineapple
Grapefruit	Plums
Honeydew	

Turkey Ham

Helpful Menu Hints

1. Keep your pancakes warm by piling them on a paper-lined baking sheet in warm oven. Place paper towels between each layer of pancakes to keep them from going soggy.

2. If you reuse syrup on another day, whisk it briskly while reheating it to remove lumps.

Food for Thought

Webster's has a great definition for the word <u>diet:</u> "regular food and drink."

Breakfast Recipes

Whole Wheat Pancakes

1	C	whole wheat flour
½	C	wheat germ
2	tsp	baking powder
½	tsp	baking soda
¼	tsp	salt
4		egg whites
2	tsp	oil
1¼	C	skim milk
3	T	apple juice concentrate (unsweetened)
1	tsp	vanilla

In large mixing bowl stir together flour, wheat germ, baking powder, baking soda, and salt. In small mixing bowl, beat eggs with fork. Beat in remaining ingredients. Add egg mixture to flour mixture. Stir mixture until blended but slightly lumpy. Pour 1/4 cup batter on griddle or skillet for each pancake; turn once, cooking on both sides.

Yield: 10 (4-inch) pancakes

	RCU	FU	Cal	%Fat	P	F	C	Na
per pancake	0	.5	196	17	11	4	31	393

Maple Syrup

2	C	water
¼	C	apple juice concentrate (unsweetened)
1½	T	maple extract

Mix together:

3	T	cornstarch
½	C	water

In medium saucepan, bring water and juice concentrate to a boil. Slowly stir in cornstarch mixture. Reduce heat. Continue stirring until mixture thickens. Add maple extract. Serve.

Yield: 1 pint or 16 (1 T) servings

	RCU	FU	Cal	%Fat	P	F	C	Na
per Tbls	0	0	25	1	T	T	6	2

Raspberry Compote

2	C	water
1	C	frozen blackberries (unsweetened)
¼	C	apple-raspberry juice concentrate (unsweetened)

In separate bowl mix:

3	T	cornstarch
½	C	water

In a medium saucepan, bring water and juice concentrate to a boil. Slowly stir in cornstarch mixture. Reduce heat, stirring constantly until mixture is thick. Add blackberries and mix well. Remove from heat.

Yield: 6 (1/2 cup) servings

	RCU	FU	Cal	%Fat	P	F	C	Na
per serving	0	0	50	3	T	T	12	3

Turkey Ham Slices

Cut turkey ham into thin slices; bake, broil, or grill slices. Serve warm.

1 serving = 3 oz.

	RCU	FU	Cal	%Fat	P	F	C	Na
per serving	0	.5	109	36	16	4	T	847

Lunch Menu Criteria

Products You'll Need

Chicken Ala King:

Boneless chicken breasts
Onions
Bell peppers
Mushrooms
Chicken bouillon granules
Onion powder
Dry mustard
Ground thyme
White pepper
Cornstarch
Skim milk
Nonfat milk powder

Rice Pilaf:

Wild Rice Pilaf mix

For Remaining Menu:

Fresh or frozen peas
Carrots
Celery
Honeydew melon
Whole wheat bread

Helpful Menu Hints

1.   To make toast points, cut toast slices into quarters, diagonally.

2.   For rice pilaf, follow package directions. For added flavor and color, stir in 1 tablespoon diced pimiento.

Food For Thought

Know what you're eating; read the label before you buy.

Lunch Recipes

Chicken Ala King

10	oz	chicken breasts, boneless, skinless, cut into 1-inch squares
2	med	onions, cut into 1-inch squares
3	med	bell peppers, cut into 1-inch squares
6	lg	mushrooms, quartered
2½	T	chicken bouillon granules
1	T	onion powder
1	tsp	dry mustard
¼	tsp	ground thyme
¼	tsp	white pepper
2	C	water

Mix together:

| 3 | T | cornstarch |
| ½ | C | water |

Mix together:

| ½ | C | skim milk |
| ¼ | C | nonfat milk powder |

In a 3-quart saucepan coated lightly with a nonstick spray, saute chicken, onions, and peppers over medium-high heat until vegetables are tender. Add spices. Blend well. Add water and bring mixture to a boil. Add cornstarch mixture, slowly stirring constantly until mixture starts to thicken. Reduce heat. Add mushrooms and milk mixture. Blend well. Continue cooking mixture on low heat an additional 10 minutes.

Yield: 6 servings

	RCU	FU	Cal	%Fat	P	F	C	Na
per serving	0	0	128	9	15	1	14	75

Wild Rice Pilaf

Prepare according to package directions.

Dinner Menu Criteria

Products You'll Need

Sauce:

Ground turkey
Onions
Bell peppers
Mushrooms
Worchestershire sauce
Liquid smoke
Onion powder
Garlic powder
Chicken bouillon granules
Beef bouillon granules
Ground oregano
Ground thyme
Ground rosemary
Ground fennel
White pepper
Tomato puree
Apple juice concentrate (unsweetened)

Salad:

Head lettuce
Tomatoes
Cucumbers

For remaining menu:

Green beans
Garlic bread sticks
Whole wheat noodles

Dressing:

Cottage cheese
Plain nonfat yogurt
Apple juice concentrate
    (unsweetened)
Chicken bouillon granules
Ground oregano
Sweet basil
Garlic powder
Onion powder
White pepper
Ground cloves
Red wine vinegar

Pie:

Grapenuts cereal
Apple juice concentrate
    (unsweetened)
Low fat cottage cheese
Pineapple juice (unsweetened)
Apple juice concentrate
    (unsweetened)
Fresh lime juice
Peppermint extract
Mint flakes
Unflavored gelatin
Skim milk

Pictured: The Gourmet Salad with Zesty Tomato Dressing, p. 102; Hot Blueberry Muffin, p. 41.

Helpful Menu Hints

1. Make the peppermint pie ahead of time; it needs to chill for six hours.

2. If you double the recipe for the sauce, you'll have enough left for pizza on Day 4 and lasagna on Day 9.

3. Follow cooking directions on the noodle package, but take care not to overcook the noodles.

Pictured: Sweet Pepper Cod, p. 236; Spinach and Mushroom Salad with Vinegar Dressing, p. 237; Steamed Zucchini and Tomato, p. 238; De-Licious Applesauce Cake, p. 239.

Food for Thought

From start to finish, timing is one golden key to a culinary success.

Dinner Recipes

Spaghetti with De-Licious Meat Sauce

½	lb	ground turkey
2	med	onions, diced
2		bell peppers, diced
6	lg	mushrooms, diced
2	T	Worchestershire sauce
⅛	tsp	liquid smoke
1	T	onion powder
1½	T	garlic powder
1	T	chicken bouillon granules
1	T	beef bouillon granules
1½	tsp	ground oregano
1	tsp	sweet basil
1	tsp	ground thyme
½	tsp	ground rosemary
¼	tsp	ground fennel
¼	tsp	white pepper
29½	oz can	tomato puree
3	T	apple juice concentrate (unsweetened)

In a medium saucepan coated lightly with a nonstick spray, saute turkey until browned. Add onion and bell pepper. Blend well. Continue cooking on medium heat until vegetables are tender. Add Worchestershire sauce, liquid smoke, and all spices and seasonings; blend well. Add mushrooms, tomato puree, and juice concentrate; blend well. Simmer for 15 minutes. Serve over whole wheat spaghetti noodles.

Yield: 6 servings

	RCU	FU	Cal	%Fat	P	F	C	Na
per serving	0	.5	354	8	26	3	58	138

Fresh Garden Salad with Italian Dressing

For salad, see recipe, Day 1, lunch.

Italian Dressing

1	C	Basic Dressing *(see recipe, Day 1, lunch)*
1	T	apple juice concentrate (unsweetened)
½	tsp	chicken bouillon granules
½	tsp	ground oregano
½	tsp	sweet basil
½	tsp	garlic powder
½	tsp	onion powder

pinch of white pepper
pinch of ground cloves

1	T	red wine vinegar

In a medium mixing bowl, gently whisk all ingredients together until blended. Chill before serving.

Yield: 6 (1/4 cup) servings

	RCU	FU	Cal	%Fat	P	F	C	Na
per serving	0	0	52	14	6	1	5	169

Godfather's Peppermint Pie

Crust:

2	C	Grapenuts cereal
2	T	apple juice concentrate (unsweetened)

In a blender, blend 1 cup Grapenuts until the mixture is fine crumbs; reserve the other cup. Pour juice concentrate evenly into a 9x9 nonstick baking pan. Pour unprocessed Grapenuts evenly into pan. Pour processed Grapenuts evenly over above mixture.

Filling:

1½	C	low fat cottage cheese
1	C	pineapple juice (unsweetened)
2	T	apple juice concentrate (unsweetened)
1	T	fresh lime juice
1	tsp	peppermint extract
½	tsp	mint flakes, ground
1	T	unflavored gelatin dissolved in small amount of skim milk

In blender, blend all ingredients until smooth. Pour over Grapenuts mixture. Chill for 6 hours before serving.

Yield: 8 (2-inch) servings

	RCU	FU	Cal	%Fat	P	F	C	Na
per serving	0	0	185	5	12	1	33	379

Gifford's

D A Y   3

BREAKFAST

PAGE 64

Chilled Quartered Honeydew Melon

Hot Cracked Wheat Cereal
with Sliced Bananas, Skim Milk, Raisins

Hot Fresh Blueberry Muffins
with Berry-Fruit Preserves

LUNCH

PAGE 66

Turkey Salad Pita Sandwich

Cup of Split Pea Soup

Tomato and Cucumber Salad

Crisp Apple Whip

DINNER

PAGE 72

Chicken Chow Mein
Served Over Turkey Ham Fried Rice

Crisp Stir-Fry Vegetables

Melon Balls in De-Lite Lemon Sauce

Breakfast Menu Criteria

Products You'll Need

Cereal and Condiments:

Cracked wheat
Skim milk
Bananas
Raisins

Honeydew melon

Preserves:

Berries (unsweetened)
Apple-raspberry concentrate
(unsweetened)
Cornstarch

Blueberry Muffins:

Whole wheat flour
Unprocessed bran
Baking powder
Baking soda
Salt
Eggs whites
Oil
Skim milk
Apple juice concentrate
  (unsweetened)
Frozen blueberries
  (unsweetened)

Helpful Menu Hints

1.   You can use the leftover cereal as a great rice substitute: simply reheat it in the microwave oven and stir in a small amount of Grapenuts cereal.

2.   To give muffins a buttery flavor, add two packets of Butter Buds to dry muffin ingredients before baking.

3.   You can also use leftover fruit compote as fruit preserves--just mix it well with a fork before serving.

Food for Thought

Attitude is a second key to success; never say "I can't."

Breakfast Recipes

Cracked Wheat Cereal

1	C	cracked wheat
2½	C	water

Bring water to a boil; add cracked wheat and stir. Reduce heat to low; cover. Cook for 12 minutes, stirring occasionally. Stir in skim milk, sliced bananas, and raisins as desired.

Yield: 4 servings

	RCU	FU	Cal	%Fat	P	F	C	Na
per serving	0	0	80	5	3	.5	18	T

Hot Blueberry Muffins

See recipe, Day 1, lunch.

Berry-Fruit Preserves

1	C	berries, unsweetened, fresh or frozen
1	C	water
3	T	apple-raspberry concentrate (unsweetened)
2	T	cornstarch

Mix water and cornstarch together in a small saucepan. Over medium heat, stirring constantly, heat until mixture thickens. Remove from heat. Add concentrate; blend well. Add berries and gently fold into mixture.

Yield: approximately 1 pint or 16 (2 T) servings

	RCU	FU	Cal	%Fat	P	F	C	Na
per serving	0	0	13	2	T	T	3	1

Lunch Menu Criteria

Products You'll Need

Sandwich:

Turkey breast, cooked
Celery
Basic Dressing (see recipe, Day 1, lunch)
Onion powder
Chicken bouillon granules
Celery seed
Rubbed sage
White pepper
Apple juice concentrate (unsweetened)
Whole wheat pita bread

Salad:

Tomatoes
Cucumber
Basic Dressing (see recipe, Day 1, lunch)
White vinegar
Dill juice
Lemon juice
Pineapple juice concentrate
(unsweetened)
Garlic powder
Onion powder
Sweet basil
Chicken bouillon granules

Soup:

Dry split peas
Onion
Celery
Potatoes
Carrots
Turkey ham
Chicken bouillon granules
Onion powder
Garlic powder
Worchestershire sauce
Liquid smoke
Skim milk
Nonfat milk powder

Apple Whip:

Apple
Apple juice concentrate
(unsweetened)
Cinnamon
Allspice
Plain nonfat yogurt
Skim milk
Nonfat milk powder

Helpful Menu Hints

1. Start the soup first, and then make salad--it needs to be chilled for an hour before serving.

2. This soup freezes well; put leftovers in the freezer in a well-sealed container.

3. Leftover dressing from the salad is delicious served over sliced garden tomatoes.

Food for Thought

Procrastination is the first enemy of change.

Lunch Recipes

Turkey Salad Pita

6	oz	turkey breast, cooked, diced medium
½		celery stalk, diced fine
½	C	Basic Dressing *(see recipe, Day 1, lunch)*
1	tsp	onion powder
¼	tsp	chicken bouillon granules
¼	tsp	celery seed

pinch of rubbed sage
dash of white pepper

1	tsp	apple juice concentrate (unsweetened)
4		whole wheat pita bread

In a small mixing bowl, blend turkey and celery together. In a separate bowl, mix remaining ingredients until smooth. Add this mixture to turkey and celery mixture; blend well. Spoon mixture into whole wheat pita pocket. Serve with crisp lettuce leaves, if desired.

Yield: 4 sandwiches

	RCU	FU	Cal	%Fat	P	F	C	Na
per sandwich	0	0	181	6	18	1	25	295

Split Pea Soup

1	lb	dry split peas
8	C	water
1	lg	onion, chopped
1	C	celery, chopped
1	C	potatoes, diced
1	C	carrots, shredded
2	oz	turkey ham, chopped
1	T	chicken bouillon granules
1	tsp	onion powder
1	tsp	garlic powder
1	tsp	Worchestershire Sauce
⅛	tsp	liquid smoke

Mix together:

½	C	skim milk
½	C	nonfat milk powder

Rinse peas; place in 3-quart saucepan. Add water, bring to a boil, stir often. Reduce heat; cover and simmer 1 1/4 hours, stirring often. In a separate saucepan coated lightly with a nonstick spray, saute onion, celery, potatoes, and carrots until onions are transparent. Mix chicken bouillon granules with 1/4 cup water; add this mixture all at once to vegetables. Blend well. Add vegetables, turkey ham, and seasonings to soup. Blend well. Simmer 30 minutes. Stir milk mixture into soup; heat through.

Yield: 8 servings

	RCU	FU	Cal	%Fat	P	F	C	Na
per serving	0	0	269	4	19	1	47	168

Tomato and Cucumber Salad

2		tomatoes, cut in wedges
1		cucumber, peeled, sliced
½	C	Basic Dressing *(see recipe, Day 1, lunch)*
1	tsp	white vinegar
1	tsp	dill juice
1	tsp	lemon juice
1	tsp	pineapple juice concentrate (unsweetened)
½	tsp	garlic powder
½	tsp	onion powder
½	tsp	sweet basil
¼	tsp	chicken bouillon granules

In a salad bowl, combine tomatoes and cucumbers. In a small mixing bowl, gently whisk remaining ingredients until blended. Pour dressing evenly over tomatoes and cucumbers; cover and refrigerate one hour. Remove tomatoes and cucumbers from dressing with a slotted spoon when serving. Pour remaining dressing over salad if desired.

Yield: 4 servings

	RCU	FU	Cal	%Fat	P	F	C	Na
per serving	0	0	72	12	6	1	11	138

Crisp Apple Whip

1		red delicious apple, cored, cut into medium pieces
2	T	apple juice concentrate (unsweetened)
1	tsp	cinnamon
¼	tsp	allspice
2	T	plain nonfat yogurt
½	C	skim milk
3	T	nonfat milk powder

In small bowl blend apple pieces, juice concentrate, cinnamon, allspice, and yogurt. Refrigerate. In mixer bowl, beat skim milk and nonfat milk powder at medium speed of electric mixer for about 2 minutes, or until soft peaks form. Gently fold this mixture into apple mixture. Serve.

Yield: 4 servings

	RCU	FU	Cal	%Fat	P	F	C	Na
per serving	0	0	82	4	4	T	17	54

Dinner Menu Criteria

Products You'll Need

Chow Mein:

Boneless chicken breasts
Onion
Bell peppers
Red peppers
Celery
Chicken bouillon granules
Onion powder
Ground ginger
Ground celery seed
Allspice
White pepper
Apple juice concentrate (unsweetened)
Kikkoman mild soy sauce
Cornstarch
Bamboo shoots (canned)
Water chestnuts (canned)
Nonfat milk powder
Bean sprouts

Fried Rice:

Brown rice
Green onion
Diced pimiento
Turkey ham
Onion powder
Fennel seed
Pepper

Stir-Fry:

Broccoli
Bell peppers
Carrots
Cauliflower
Celery
Mushrooms
Onions
Lemon juice
Kikkoman mild soy sauce

Melon Balls With Lemon Sauce:

Assorted melon balls, frozen (unsweetened)
Plain nonfat yogurt
Pineapple-orange-banana juice concentrate (unsweetened)
Lemon peel (Schilling)
Vanilla

Helpful Menu Hints

1. Don't let the number of ingredients in this menu overwhelm you--it's really very simple to prepare.

2. For the fried rice, use leftover rice from Day 2's lunch (if there is any). If you don't have any leftover rice, prepare the rice first, since it will take the longest.

3. Save time by preparing all the vegetables for this menu at the same time.

Food for Thought

You only fail if you fail to try.

Dinner Recipes

Fried Rice

2	C	cooked brown rice
½	C	green onion, sliced thin
1	T	diced pimiento
1	oz	turkey ham, chopped
1	tsp	onion powder
½	tsp	fennel seed

pepper to taste

In a skillet sprayed lightly with a nonstick spray, saute green onion, pimiento, and turkey ham until heated through. Add cooked rice and spices; blend well. Saute for 5 minutes, stirring frequently.

Yield: 4 servings

	RCU	FU	Cal	%Fat	P	F	C	Na
per serving	0	0	123	7	4	1	24	319

Chicken Chow Mein

10	oz	boneless chicken breasts, skinned, cut into 1-inch squares
1	lg	onion, cut into 1-inch squares
2		bell peppers, cut into 1-inch squares
1		red pepper, cut into 1-inch squares
2		celery stalks, cut into 1/2-inch slices
2	C	water
2½	tsp	chicken bouillon granules
2	tsp	onion powder
½	tsp	ground ginger
½	tsp	ground celery seed
¼	tsp	allspice

white pepper to taste

2	T	apple juice concentrate (unsweetened)
4	T	Kikkoman mild soy sauce

Mix together:

| 3 | T | cornstarch |
| ½ | C | water |

1	sm can	bamboo shoots, with juice
1	sm can	water chestnuts, sliced, with juice
1	T	nonfat milk powder
3	oz	bean sprouts

In a 3-quart saucepan sprayed lightly with a nonstick spray, saute chicken, onions, peppers, and celery until chicken is cooked through and vegetables are tender. Add water all at once and stir well. Add spices; stir. Add juice concentrate and soy sauce; stir. Bring mixture to a boil. Add cornstarch mixture slowly, stirring constantly until mixture begins to thicken. Reduce heat and simmer 10 minutes. Drain juice from bamboo shoots and water chestnuts; reserve for later. Add bamboo shoots, water chestnuts, and bean sprouts to mixture; blend well. Mix nonfat milk powder with a small amount of reserved juice and stir into mixture. Save remaining juice for stir-fry vegetables.

Note: Kikkoman mild soy sauce is extremely low in sodium.

Yield: 4 servings

	RCU	FU	Cal	%Fat	P	F	C	Na
per serving	0	0	201	7	22	2	26	585

Crisp Stir-Fry Vegetables

1	C	broccoli, cut thin diagonally
1	C	bell pepper, cut julienne
1	C	carrots, cut thin diagonally
1	C	cauliflower, cut thin diagonally
1	C	celery, cut thin diagonally
1	C	mushrooms, sliced
1	C	onions, cut julienne
1	C	juice of bamboo shoots and water chestnuts
1	T	lemon juice

Kikkoman mild soy sauce to taste

Preheat a large skillet or wok; spray lightly with a nonstick spray. Place all vegetables in skillet or wok; stir-fry until vegetables are crisp-tender. Add juices and soy sauce while stir-frying for flavor.

Yield: 4 generous servings

	RCU	FU	Cal	%Fat	P	F	C	Na
per serving	0	0	57	8	3	T	12	225

Melon Balls in De-Lite Lemon Sauce

1	lb bag	assorted melon balls, frozen, unsweetened
1	C	plain nonfat yogurt
2	T	pineapple-orange-banana juice concentrate (unsweetened)
1	T	lemon peel (Schilling)
½	tsp	vanilla

Distribute melon balls evenly into dessert dishes; allow to thaw at room temperature. In small mixing bowl, gently whisk remaining ingredients until blended. Pour over melon balls. Garnish with fresh lemon slice and a sprig of fresh mint.

Yield: 4 servings

	RCU	FU	Cal	%Fat	P	F	C	Na
per serving	0	0	86	4	4	T	17	77

Gifford's

DAY 4

BREKAFAST

PAGE 80

Denver Omelet

Baked Homestyle Hashbrowns

Gourmet De-Lites Ketchup

Chilled Quartered Cantaloupe

Whole-Grain Toast
with Preserves

LUNCH

PAGE 84

Gourmet Pita Pizza

Assorted Green Salad
with Fresh Tomato Slices
served with
Pineapple Oregano Dressing

DINNER

PAGE 87

Baked Meatloaf with Rich Brown Gravy

Stuffed Potato

Fresh Steamed Broccoli

Hot Buttermilk Muffin

Banana-Pineapple Pudding

Breakfast Menu Criteria

Products You'll Need

Omelet:

Eggs
Chicken bouillon granules
Pepper
Turkey ham
Onion
Bell pepper

Remaining Menu:

Cantaloupe
Whole-grain bread

Preserves:

(see recipe, Day 3, breakfast)

Potatoes:

Russet potatoes
Onion powder
Pepper

Ketchup:

Tomato puree
Apple juice concentrate
  (unsweetened)
White wine vinegar
Worchestershire sauce
Dill pickle juice
Beef bouillon granules
Onion powder
Garlic powder
Dill weed
Dry mustard
Turmeric
White pepper
Cloves

Helpful Menu Hints

1.   Use any leftover egg mixture in meatloaf or muffins.

2.   All three menus for this day call for onions and bell peppers; if possible, prepare enough for all three menus at the same time.

3.   Store ketchup in a screw-top jar; shake or stir the ketchup well before using it again.

Food for Thought

According to Webster's, habitual means "constantly practiced; customary; regular."

Breakfast Recipes

Denver Omelet

2	lg	eggs
4		egg whites (at room temperature)
½	tsp	chicken bouillon granules
2	T	water

pinch of pepper

Saute together until cooked through:

1	oz	turkey ham
1	oz	onion, diced
1	oz	bell pepper, diced

In a small mixing bowl, beat eggs, egg whites, chicken granules, water, and pepper until smooth and fluffy. Spray an omelet or small saute pan with a nonstick spray. Place over medium heat. Ladle half of egg mixture into pan and roll pan side to side until mixture covers pan. Reduce heat to low. Gently push one corner of egg mixture inward 1 inch and tilt pan toward you, enough to let remaining egg liquid roll out into pan to cover again. Place sauteed turkey ham, onion, and pepper mixture in center of omelet. Fold 1/2 of omelet towards you to cover filling. Place spatula underneath omelet and fold over. Remove to serving dish. Repeat procedure for second omelet.

Yield: 2 servings

	RCU	FU	Cal	%Fat	P	F	C	Na
per serving	0	1	137	42	16	6	3	312

Baked Homestyle Hashbrowns

2	lg	russet potatoes, diced
4	C	water
1	T	onion powder

pepper to taste

In a medium saucepan, bring potatoes and water to a boil. Reduce heat and simmer until potatoes are cooked through. Remove from heat. Drain. Spray a baking dish with a nonstick spray. Spread potatoes evenly in baking dish. Season with onion powder and pepper. Bake in preheated oven at 400° for 15 minutes.

Yield: 4 servings

	RCU	FU	Cal	%Fat	P	F	C	Na
per serving	0	0	71	1	2	T	16	6

Gourmet De-Lites Ketchup

2	C	tomato puree
3	T	apple juice concentrate (unsweetened)
1½	T	white wine vinegar
1½	T	Worchestershire sauce
1½	T	dill pickle juice
1	T	beef bouillon granules
2	tsp	onion powder
1	tsp	garlic powder
½	tsp	dill weed
½	tsp	dry mustard
¼	tsp	turmeric

pinch of white pepper
pinch of clove

In a mixing bowl, blend all ingredients using a wire whisk.

Yield: 1 1/2 pints or 24 (1 T) servings

	RCU	FU	Cal	%Fat	P	F	C	Na
per tablespoon	0	0	9	4	T	T	2	9

Berry-Fruit Preserves

See recipe, Day 3, breakfast.

Lunch Menu Criteria

Products You'll Need

Pizza:

Spaghetti sauce
(see recipe, Day 2, dinner)
Tomato puree
Bell pepper
Tomatoes
Onions
Mushrooms
Zucchini
Mozzarella cheese, part skim
Whole wheat pita bread
Oregano

Salad:

Head lettuce
Leaf lettuce
Tomatoes

Dressing:

Plain nonfat yogurt
Crushed pineapple
   (unsweetened)
Chicken bouillon granules
Oregano
Garlic powder
Onion powder
White pepper

Helpful Menu Hints

1.   Planning ahead? Make pita pizzas to freeze while preparing spaghetti dinner.

2.   If you freeze pita pizzas, wrap them tightly individually and allow them to thaw before cooking.

3.   In a hurry? Pizzas can be microwaved on high for 2 1/2 minutes.

Food for Thought

The average American diet contains 40 to 50 percent fat.

Lunch Recipes

Gourmet Pita Pizza

2	C	spaghetti sauce *(see recipe, Day 2, dinner)*
½	C	tomato puree
1	C	bell pepper, diced
1	C	tomatoes, diced
1	C	onions, diced
1	C	mushrooms, diced
1	C	zucchini, diced
1	C	shredded mozzarella cheese, part skim
6		whole wheat pita bread slices
1	T	oregano

In a blender, combine spaghetti sauce and tomato puree; blend until smooth. In a large mixing bowl, combine vegetables and tomatoes. Blend well. Coat a cookie sheet with a nonstick spray. Place pita bread slices on cookie sheet. Ladle approximately 2 ounces of sauce in center of bread and spread in a circle until sauce covers bread. Spoon vegetables and tomatoes over each pita slice, distributing as evenly as possible. Sprinkle cheese evenly over each pizza. Top with any remaining sauce. Bake in preheated oven at 425° for 15 minutes, or until crust of pita bread is golden brown. Sprinkle oregano over each pizza slice 5 minutes before removing from oven.

Yield: 6 pita pizzas

	RCU	FU	Cal	%Fat	P	F	C	Na
per pizza	0	1	288	25	21	8	38	418

Assorted Green Salad with Fresh Tomato Slices

1	head	iceberg lettuce
1	head	leaf lettuce (red, green, or romaine)
2		tomatoes, sliced

Remove outer leaves of iceberg lettuce head. Discard any wilted or discolored outer leaves. Hit stem end sharply on tabletop to loosen core. Twist and remove core. Place lettuce head bottom side up, under cold water, and rinse well. Invert lettuce head and let water drain thoroughly. Place in plastic bag; refrigerate a few hours to crisp. For leaf lettuce, carefully wash and store each individual leaf in a plastic bag.

Tear lettuce leaves into pieces and place in salad bowl. (Chopping lettuce with a knife bruises the leaves.)

Yield: approximately 8 servings

	RCU	FU	Cal	%Fat	P	F	C	Na
per serving	0	0	43	3	3	T	7	44

Pineapple Oregano Dressing

1	C	nonfat plain yogurt
3	T	crushed pineapple, drained (unsweetened); reserve liquid
1	T	reserved pineapple juice
½	tsp	chicken bouillon granules
½	tsp	oregano
¼	tsp	garlic powder
¼	tsp	onion powder
pinch of white pepper		

In a small mixing bowl, gently whisk ingredients until blended well.

Yield: 1 cup or 4 (1/4 cup) servings

	RCU	FU	Cal	%Fat	P	F	C	Na
per serving	0	0	43	3	3	T	7	44

Dinner Menu Criteria

Products You'll Need

Meatloaf:

Ground turkey
Onion
Celery
Mushrooms
Grapenuts cereal
Beef bouillon granules
Onion powder
Garlic powder
Ground thyme
White pepper
Gourmet De-Lites Ketchup
(see recipe, Day 4, breakfast)
Worchestershire sauce
Liquid smoke

Potatoes:

Russet potatoes
Green onion
Chicken bouillon granules
Onion powder
Butter Buds
White pepper
Skim milk
Nonfat milk powder
Mozzarella cheese, part skim

Gravy:

Beef bouillon granules
Onion powder
Kitchen Bouquet

Muffins:

Whole wheat flour
Buttermilk powder
Baking powder
Baking soda
Salt
Apple juice concentrate
    (unsweetened)
Egg whites
Oil

Pudding:

Bananas
Crushed pineapple
    (unsweetened)
Pineapple juice concentrate
    (unsweetened)
Skim milk
Vanilla
Almond extract
Cornstarch

Helpful Menu Hints

1. It's easier to form a meatloaf if you put a small amount of water on your hands before working with the meat.

2. Leftover meatloaf is great for sandwiches.

3. It's best to spoon the potato flesh while the potatoes are hot. Use a towel to handle the potato while spooning.

Pictured: Cinnamon French-Style Toast, p. 98; Blackberry Compote, p. 35; Seasoned Turkey Sausage, p. 99.

Food for Thought

The average American consumes about 125 pounds of sugar per year.

Dinner Recipes

Baked Meatloaf with Rich Brown Gravy

1	lb	ground turkey
1	sm	onion, finely diced
2		celery stalks, finely diced
6	med	mushrooms, finely diced
1	C	Grapenuts cereal, finely crushed
1	T	beef bouillon granules
1	T	onion powder
1	tsp	garlic powder
½	tsp	ground thyme
¼	tsp	white pepper
¼	C	Gourmet De-Lites Ketchup *(see recipe, Day 4, breakfast)*
1	T	Worchestershire sauce
¼	tsp	liquid smoke
1		egg
1		egg white

Preheat oven to 400°. In a large mixing bowl, mix all ingredients well. Coat a 13x9x2 baking pan with a nonstick spray. Place mixture into pan and form a roll from end to end. Add 1 cup water to pan and bake, covered, for 40 minutes. Remove cover and bake an additional 15 minutes to brown. Remove from oven; drain juice from pan into saucepan for gravy.

Yield: 4 servings

	RCU	FU	Cal	%Fat	P	F	C	Na
per serving	0	1	298	16	32	5	30	368

Pictured: The Gourmet Burger, p. 138; Baked Steak Fries, p. 139; Gourmet De-Lites Ketchup, p. 83; Creamy Boysenberry Shake, p. 140.

Rich Brown Gravy

Add to juice in saucepan from meatloaf:

1	C	water
1½	tsp	beef bouillon granules
1	tsp	onion powder
½	tsp	Kitchen Bouquet

Bring ingredients to a boil. Reduce heat to simmer. Mix 2 tablespoons cornstarch with 1/4 cup water; add slowly to mixture, stirring constantly, until gravy thickens. Add 1 teaspoon paprika to gravy for color. Ladle over meatloaf.

Yield: 6 (1/4 cup) servings

	RCU	FU	Cal	%Fat	P	F	C	Na
per serving	0	0	19	16	.3	T	4	199

Baked Stuffed Potato

4	lg	russet potatoes
1		green onion, thinly sliced
1	tsp	chicken bouillon granules
1	tsp	onion powder
1	pkg	Butter Buds
white pepper to taste		
½	C	skim milk
¼	C	nonfat milk powder
2	oz	shredded mozzarella cheese, part skim

Preheat oven to 400°. Bake potatoes for 1 1/4 hours. Remove from oven. Cut potatoes into halves lengthwise. Spoon out potato flesh and place in medium mixing bowl; reserve potato shells. Add onion and spices. With electric mixer, mix potato mixture on medium speed for 30 seconds. Heat milk. Continue mixing potato mixture on low speed. Add milk slowly until well blended. Whip potatoes on high speed 30 seconds. Spoon potato mixture into reserved potato shells. Place stuffed potatoes on baking sheet. Sprinkle mozzarella cheese on top of potatoes. Place potatoes in oven until cheese is melted.

Yield: 8 servings

	RCU	FU	Cal	%Fat	P	F	C	Na
per serving	0	0	105	11	7	1	17	74

Hot Buttermilk Muffins

1½	C	whole wheat flour
8	T	buttermilk powder
1½	tsp	baking powder
½	tsp	baking soda
¼	tsp	salt
2	T	apple juice concentrate (unsweetened)
2		egg whites
1	C	water
1	tsp	oil

In a medium bowl, mix dry ingredients together. Form a well in center of mixture. In a separate mixing bowl, beat egg whites until smooth. Add remaining ingredients; beat until smooth. Pour egg mixture into well of flour mixture. Stir mixture just until moistened. Mixture should appear lumpy. Coat a nonstick muffin pan lightly with a nonstick spray. Fill muffin cups 2/3 full to allow space for rising. Bake in 400° oven for 20 minutes or until golden brown.

Yield: 12 muffins

	RCU	FU	Cal	%Fat	P	F	C	Na
per muffin	0	0	81	11	4	1	15	155

Banana-Pineapple Pudding

2	lg	bananas, ripe
3	T	crushed pineapple, unsweetened, with juice
3	T	pineapple juice concentrate (unsweetened)
1	C	skim milk
½	tsp	vanilla
2	drps	almond extract
5	T	cornstarch

Place all ingredients in blender. Mix on high speed until smooth. Pour mixture into saucepan. Cook mixture over medium heat, stirring constantly until thickened, about 10 minutes. Pour mixture evenly into dessert dishes. Serve warm or chilled.

Yield: 5 servings

	RCU	FU	Cal	%Fat	P	F	C	Na
per serving	0	0	129	3	3	T	30	26

Gifford's

D A Y 5

BREAKFAST

PAGE 96

Chilled Apple Slices

*Cinnamon French-Style Toast
with Blackberry Compote
or Apple-Butter Syrup*

Seasoned Turkey Sausage

LUNCH

PAGE 100

The Gourmet Salad

*Hot Blueberry Muffins
with Raspberry Preserves*

Piece of Fresh Fruit

DINNER

PAGE 104

*Baked Tarragon Chicken
with
Bearnaise Sauce*

Brown Rice Pilaf with Mushrooms

Steamed Brussels Sprouts

Tomato and Cottage Cheese Salad

Lemon Fluff Parfait

Breakfast Menu Criteria

Products You'll Need

French Toast:

Eggs
Apple juice concentrate
(unsweetened)
Vanilla
Almond extract
Skim milk
Whole wheat flour
Baking powder
Cinnamon
Whole wheat bread

Blackberry Compote:

(see recipe, Day 1, breakfast)

Apple-Butter Syrup:

Apple juice concentrate
(unsweetened)
Butter Buds
Cornstarch

Sausage:

Ground turkey
Chicken bouillon granules
Rubbed sage
Onion powder
Ground caraway
Ground fennel
Paprika
Grapenuts cereal
Apple juice concentrate
(unsweetened)

Helpful Menu Hints

1. Leftover French toast should be wrapped well for storage--and it can be microwaved for a speedy breakfast!

2. Place apple slices in a mixture of water and lemon juice to prevent discoloration.

3. To save time, make extra sausage patties. Separate each pattie with waxed paper, stack four patties, wrap well, and freeze.

Food for Thought

Missing meals and eating on an irregular schedule will trigger your starvation defenses and often raises the setpoint.

Breakfast Recipes

Cinnamon French-Style Toast

2		eggs
4		egg whites, at room temperature
3	T	apple juice concentrate (unsweetened)
1	tsp	vanilla
½	tsp	almond extract
1	C	skim milk
⅔	C	whole wheat flour
1½	tsp	baking powder
2	tsp	ground cinnamon
8	slices	whole wheat bread

In a medium mixing bowl, beat egg whites until smooth. Add eggs, juice concentrate, skim milk, vanilla, and almond extract. Blend well. Add flour, baking powder, and cinnamon to egg mixture. Beat until mixture is smooth and fluffy. Coat a griddle or large skillet with a nonstick spray. Place over medium heat until hot. Dip bread in batter until soaked through. Cook until golden brown on both sides.

Yield: 4 servings

	RCU	FU	Cal	%Fat	P	F	C	Na
per serving	0	1	287	15	16	5	47	479

Blackberry Compote

See recipe, Day 1, breakfast.

Apple-Butter Syrup

2	C	water
¼	C	apple juice concentrate (unsweetened)
2	pkt	Butter Buds

Mix together:

| 3 | T | cornstarch |
| 1/2 | C | water |

In medium saucepan, bring water and juice concentrate to a boil. Slowly stir in cornstarch mixture. Reduce heat. Continue stirring until mixture thickens. Add But-ter Buds. Serve.

Yield: 1 pint or 16 (1 T) servings

	RCU	FU	Cal	%Fat	P	F	C	Na
per tablespoon	0	0	25	1	T	T	6	2

Seasoned Turkey Sausage

½	lb	ground turkey
1	tsp	chicken bouillon granules
1	tsp	rubbed sage
1	tsp	onion powder
¼	tsp	ground caraway
¼	tsp	ground fennel
¼	tsp	paprika
2	tsp	Grapenuts cereal, finely crushed
1	tsp	apple juice concentrate (unsweetened)

In a medium mixing bowl, blend all ingredients well. Coat a griddle or skillet lightly with a nonstick spray. Form sausage into 4 (2-ounce) patties. Cook patties over medium heat until golden brown on both sides.

Yield: 4 (2-ounce) servings

	RCU	FU	Cal	%Fat	P	F	C	Na
per serving	0	0	78	20	13	2	2	50

Lunch Menu Criteria

Products You'll Need

Salad:

Head lettuce
Chicken breast
Turkey ham
Lite American cheese
Mozzarella cheese, part skim
Assorted fresh vegetables

Raspberry Preserves:

Raspberries (unsweetened)
Apple-raspberry concentrate
(unsweetened)
Cornstarch

Assorted Fresh fruit:

(your choice)

Tomato Dressing:

Tomato
V-8 juice
Apple juice concentrate
  (unsweetened)
Lemon juice
Basil

Muffins:

See recipe, Day 1, lunch

Helpful Menu Hints

1.   Always check the next day's menu when you start food preparation--there might be something you can do today that will save you time tomorrow.

2.   Try to memorize preparation procedures for each menu. They will become easier each time you repeat them.

3.   If you have a problem with a meal, take notes; it will help you avoid the problem next time you prepare that recipe.

Food for Thought

To maintain health, it's recommended that you drink 2 quarts of water daily. One way to get enough water is to drink water with your meals each day.

Lunch Recipes

The Gourmet Salad

8	oz	fresh garden salad *(see recipe, Day 1, lunch)*
2	oz	boneless chicken breast, skinned, cooked, cut julienne
2	oz	turkey ham, cut julienne
2	oz	Lite American cheese, cut julienne
2	oz	mozzarella cheese, part skim, cut julienne

assorted fresh vegetables

On a salad platter, arrange 4 ounces of garden salad evenly. Place 1 ounce chicken breast, 1 ounce American cheese, 1 ounce turkey ham, and 1 ounce mozzarella cheese decoratively on top of lettuce. Garnish fresh vegetables around salad. Repeat procedure for second salad.

Yield: 2 servings

	RCU	FU	Cal	%Fat	P	F	C	Na
per serving	0	1.5	235	34	28	9	10	1068

Zesty Tomato Dressing

1	med	tomato, stem removed, quartered
1	6 oz can	V-8 juice
1	T	apple juice concentrate (unsweetened)
1	tsp	lemon juice
½	tsp	basil

In a blender, blend all ingredients on high speed for 30 seconds.

Yield: 6 (1/4 cup) servings

	RCU	FU	Cal	%Fat	P	F	C	Na
per serving	0	0	18	6	T	T	4	106

Hot Blueberry Muffins

See recipe, Day 1, lunch.

Raspberry Preserves

1	C	raspberries, unsweetened, fresh or frozen
1	C	water
3	T	apple-raspberry concentrate (unsweetened)
2	T	cornstarch

Mix water and cornstarch together in a small saucepan. Over medium heat, stirring constantly, heat until mixture thickens. Remove from heat. Add concentrate; blend well. Add raspberries and gently fold into mixture.

Yield: approximately 1 pint or 16 (2 T) servings

	RCU	FU	Cal	%Fat	P	F	C	Na
per serving	0	0	80	5	3	.5	18	T

Dinner Menu Criteria

Products You'll Need

Chicken:

Chicken breast tenders
Pineapple juice concentrate (unsweetened)
Chicken bouillon granules
Onion powder
Tarragon leaves, crushed

Bearnaise Sauce:

Tarragon wine vinegar
Tarragon leaves, crushed
Chicken bouillon granules
Onion powder
Lime juice
Cornstarch
Skim milk
Nonfat milk powder

Remaining Menu:

Brussels sprouts

Rice Pilaf:

Wild Rice Pilaf mix
Mushrooms

Tomato Cottage Cheese Salad:

Red leaf lettuce
Tomatoes
Low fat cottage cheese

Lemon Fluff Parfait:

Skim milk
Nonfat milk powder
Cornstarch
Pineapple juice concentrate
    (unsweetened)
Lemon juice
Lemon peel
Plain nonfat yogurt
Grapenuts cereal

Helpful Menu Hints

1. For time-saving meal preparation, make the dessert first, the rice second, and the chicken third.

2. This is a nice menu to feature if you're having company for dinner.

3. For a nice touch, enjoy this meal by candlelight.

Food for Thought

The only way fat can be removed from fat cells is to be burned in the muscles for energy. That makes "diet and exercise" a good marriage!

Dinner Recipes

Baked Tarragon Chicken with Bearnaise Sauce

1	lb	chicken breast tenders
2	C	water
1	T	pineapple juice concentrate (unsweetened)
2	tsp	chicken bouillon granules
1	tsp	onion powder
1	tsp	tarragon leaves, crushed

Place chicken tenders loosely in a large baking dish; make sure they are slightly separated from each other. In a small mixing bowl, blend remaining ingredients into water. Pour over chicken. Bake, uncovered, at 375° for 30 minutes.

Sauce Ingredients:

liquid from chicken

¼	C	tarragon wine vinegar
1	tsp	tarragon leaves, crushed
1	tsp	chicken bouillon granules
1	tsp	onion powder
1	tsp	lime juice

Mix together:

3	T	cornstarch
½	C	water

Mix together:

½	C	skim milk
¼	C	nonfat milk powder

In a small saucepan, combine tarragon wine vinegar and tarragon leaves. Bring to a boil and allow vinegar to boil out (evaporate), leaving only tarragon leaves. Remove from heat. Remove chicken from oven. Drain liquid into medium saucepan. Set chicken aside. Bring liquid to a boil. Add tarragon leaves, chicken bouillon granules, onion powder, and lime juice. Reduce heat to simmer. Add cornstarch mixture slowly, stirring constantly, until sauce thickens. Add milk; stir.

Pour sauce over chicken. Return chicken to oven and bake an additional 15 minutes at 375°.

Yield: 4 servings

	RCU	FU	Cal	%Fat	P	F	C	Na
per serving	0	0	200	7	30	2	15	133

Brown Rice Pilaf with Mushrooms

Follow package directions of Wild Rice Pilaf mix; add sauteed mushroom slices while rice is cooking.

Tomato and Cottage Cheese Salad

8		red leaf lettuce leaves
2		tomatoes, quartered
1	C	low fat cottage cheese

Clean lettuce leaves thoroughly. Place 2 lettuce leaves each on four salad plates, across from each other. Scoop 1/4 cup cottage cheese in center of each plate. Place 2 tomato quarters opposite lettuce leaves on each plate. If desired, sprinkle paprika over cottage cheese for color.

Yield: 4 servings

	RCU	FU	Cal	%Fat	P	F	C	Na
per serving	0	0	88	16	10	2	10	246

Lemon Fluff Parfait

1	C	skim milk
½	C	nonfat milk powder
5	T	cornstarch
3	T	pineapple juice concentrate (unsweetened)
2	T	lemon juice
2	T	lemon peel
¼	C	plain nonfat yogurt
¼	C	Grapenuts cereal, crushed

Combine skim milk, nonfat milk powder, cornstarch, pineapple juice concentrate, and lemon juice in blender. Blend on high speed 30 seconds. Pour mixture into medium saucepan. Cook over medium heat, stirring constantly, until mixture thickens. Remove from heat and allow to cool. Add yogurt to cooled mixture and whip with wire whisk until well blended. Sprinkle Grapenut cereal crumbs in parfait glasses; next, spoon small amount of parfait into each glass. Sprinkle small amount of lemon peel over parfait mixture. Repeat procedure to make three layers. Garnish with a thin lemon slice. Refrigerate 1 hour before serving.

Yield: 4 servings

	RCU	FU	Cal	%Fat	P	F	C	Na
per serving	0	0	174	2	9	T	34	173

Gifford's

D A Y 6

BREAKFAST

PAGE 112

Sunrise Orange Surprise
with Cottage Cheese

Hot Old-Fashioned Oatmeal

Sliced Bananas and Raisins

Skim Milk

Whole Wheat Toast with Preserves

LUNCH

PAGE 114

Boston Clam Chowder

Tuna Salad Sandwich
on Whole-Grain Bread

Creamy Cole Slaw Salad

Fruit Cup with Mint-Raisin Topping

DINNER

PAGE 119

Poached Red Snapper
with Dill-Tomato Sauce

Fresh Spinach Salad
with Apple-Nut Dressing

Seasoned Noodles

Fried Zucchini
with Mushrooms and Onions

Berries Melange Dessert

Breakfast Menu Criteria

Products You'll Need

Orange Surprise:

Oranges
Low fat cottage cheese
Orange peel (Schilling)
Orange juice concentrate (unsweetened)
Nutmeg

Oatmeal:

Old-fashioned oats
Bananas
Raisins
Skim milk

Preserves/Toast:

See recipe, Day 3, breakfast
Whole wheat bread

Helpful Menu Hints

1.   This menu is perfect for days when you're in a hurry!

2.   For variety, use pineapple and pineapple juice concentrate instead of oranges and orange juice concentrate.

3.   You can make a "mock honey" by mixing equal amounts of apple juice concentrate and pineapple juice concentrate; try drizzling some over your oatmeal.

Food for Thought

Nothing tastes as good as being thin feels!

Breakfast Recipes

Sunrise Orange Surprise with Cottage Cheese

2		oranges, peeled and sectioned
½	C	low fat cottage cheese
1	T	orange peel
1	T	orange juice concentrate (unsweetened)
dash of nutmeg		

Place 1/4 cup cottage cheese in the center of a small serving plate. Place 1/2 of sectioned orange pieces around cottage cheese. Pour 1/2 of orange juice concentrate over cottage cheese, and sprinkle 1/2 of orange peel over mixture. Top with nutmeg. Repeat for second serving.

Yield: 2 servings

	RCU	FU	Cal	%Fat	P	F	C	Na
per serving	0	0	165	7	10	1	31	233

Hot Old-Fashioned Oatmeal

Follow directions on oatmeal package for preparing oatmeal. Serve with skim milk, raisins, and sliced bananas.

1 cup servings

	RCU	FU	Cal	%Fat	P	F	C	Na
per serving	0	0	145	12	6	2	25	2

Berry-Fruit Preserves

See recipe, Day 3, breakfast.

Lunch Menu Criteria

Products You'll Need

Chowder:

Onions
Celery
Potatoes
Fish bouillon granules
Chicken bouillon granules
Onion powder
Ground fennel seed
Basil
White pepper
Tabasco sauce
Liquid smoke
Cornstarch
Butter Buds
Lemon juice
Lime juice
Skim milk
Nonfat milk powder
Chopped clams

Fruit Cup:

Apple, red and green
Orange
Banana
Seedless grapes
Pineapple chunks with liquid
Apple juice concentrate (unsweetened)
Raisins
Mint flakes
Anise

Tuna Salad Sandwich:

Tuna, packed in water
Celery
Basic Dressing
(see recipe, Day 1, lunch)
Chicken bouillon granules
Onion powder
Celery seed
Dill weed
Dill pickle juice
Lemon juice
Whole wheat bread
Lettuce leaves

Cole Slaw:

Green cabbage
Plain nonfat yogurt
Pineapple juice concentrate
    (unsweetened)
Cider vinegar

Helpful Menu Hints

1. Start the chowder first; while it's simmering, you should be able to complete other menu items.

2. For a tasty change of pace from tuna salad sandwiches, try a tuna melt. Place tuna salad on a slice of bread, top with a slice of mozzarella cheese, and bake, open-faced, at 375° for 7 minutes.

Food for Thought

Your food temptations might really be food addictions--they have the same characteristics.

Lunch Recipes

Boston Clam Chowder

3	C	water
1	C	onion, diced
1	C	celery, diced
2	C	potatoes, diced
2	T	fish bouillon granules
2	tsp	chicken bouillon granules
2	tsp	onion powder
½	tsp	ground fennel seed
½	tsp	basil
⅛	tsp	white pepper
4	drp	tabasco sauce
2	drp	liquid smoke

Mix together:

3	T	cornstarch
½	C	water
2	pkt	Butter Buds
1	T	lemon juice
1	tsp	lime juice

Mix together:

1	C	skim milk
½	C	nonfat milk powder
1	C	chopped clams

In a medium saucepan coated lightly with a nonstick spray, saute vegetables over medium heat until onions are transparent. Add water all at once, and stir well. Add fish and chicken granules, spices, tabasco, and liquid smoke. Bring to a boil. Add cornstarch mixture slowly, stirring constantly. Reduce heat to simmer. Add Butter Buds, lemon juice, and lime juice. Blend well. Simmer 20 minutes, stirring often. Add milk and clams. Blend well. Simmer 10 minutes, stirring frequently.

Yield: 4 servings

	RCU	FU	Cal	%Fat	P	F	C	Na
per serving	0	0	194	3	11	1	36	396

Tuna Salad Sandwiches

6½	oz	can tuna, packed in water, drained
1		celery stalk, finely diced
½	C	Basic Dressing *(see recipe, Day 1, lunch)*
1	tsp	chicken bouillon granules
1	tsp	onion powder
½	tsp	celery seed
¼	tsp	dill weed
1	T	dill pickle juice
1	tsp	lemon juice
8	sl	whole wheat bread

In a medium bowl, combine all ingredients except bread. Blend well. Serve on whole wheat bread and garnish with lettuce leaves if desired.

Yield: tuna salad for 4 sandwiches

	RCU	FU	Cal	%Fat	P	F	C	Na
per sandwich	0	0	201	11	22	2	24	385

Creamy Cole Slaw Salad

2	C	green cabbage, shredded
½	C	plain nonfat yogurt
3	T	pineapple juice concentrate (unsweetened)
1	tsp	cider vinegar

In a medium mixing bowl, combine all ingredients; blend well. Serve on salad plate. If desired, garnish with orange curls, carrot curls, or pineapple slices.

Yield: 4 servings

	RCU	FU	Cal	%Fat	P	F	C	Na
per serving	0	0	49	2	2	T	10	29

Fruit Cup with Mint-Raisin Topping

1		red apple, cored, cut into 1/2-inch pieces
1		green apple, cored, cut into 1/2-inch pieces
1		orange, peeled, cut into 1/2-inch pieces
1		banana, sliced
1	C	seedless grapes
1	C	pineapple chunks, drained; reserve liquid
2	T	apple juice concentrate (unsweetened)
½	C	raisins
1	tsp	mint flakes
¼	tsp	anise

In a medium mixing bowl, combine apples, orange, banana, grapes, and pineapple. Stir gently until blended. In blender, combine reserved pineapple juice, apple juice concentrate, raisins, mint, and anise. Blend on high speed for 15 seconds. Spoon fruit into 4 dessert dishes. Ladle mint-raisin topping over fruit. Garnish with a sprig of fresh mint leaf, if desired.

Yield: 4 servings

	RCU	FU	Cal	%Fat	P	F	C	Na
per serving	0	0	251	3	2	1	65	8

Dinner Menu Criteria

Products You'll Need

Snapper:

Red snapper fillets
Onion
Celery
Lemon
Tomato sauce
Dill weed
Onion powder
Chicken bouillon granules
Thyme
Garlic powder
White pepper

Zucchini:

Zucchini
Mushrooms
Onion

Melange:

Raspberries, fresh or frozen
Boysenberries, fresh or frozen
Strawberries, fresh or frozen
Apple-raspberry concentrate
(unsweetened)
Plain nonfat yogurt
Vanilla
Cherry extract

Salad:

Fresh spinach leaves
Mushrooms
Red apple
Basic Dressing
(see recipe, Day 1, lunch)
Apple juice concentrate
   (unsweetened)
Chicken bouillon granules
Apple cider vinegar
Grapenuts cereal

Seasoned Noodles:

Whole wheat noodles
Butter Buds
Onion powder
Garlic powder
Black pepper

Helpful Menu Hints

1. The melange dressing needs to chill for an hour, so prepare it first.

2. Leftover noodles can be used in any soup; if you're in a hurry, you can also use leftover noodles as a substitute for rice.

Food for Thought

Don't expect instant gratification; for a boost, break large goals into smaller ones, and you'll see greater progress.

Dinner Recipes

Poached Red Snapper with Dill-Tomato Sauce

1	lb	fresh red snapper fillets
1	lg	onion, cut julienne
2		celery stalks, cut julienne

juice of 1 lemon

1	C	tomato sauce
1	tsp	dill weed
1	tsp	onion powder
1	tsp	chicken bouillon granules
½	tsp	thyme
½	tsp	garlic powder

dash of white pepper

Coat a large saucepan with a nonstick spray. Over medium heat, saute onions and celery until onions are transparent. Place red snapper fillets evenly over onions and celery. Squeeze lemon juice evenly over fillets. Cover and poach on medium heat for 10 minutes. Blend all spices with tomato sauce. Remove cover from pan. Pour tomato sauce evenly over fillets. Cover and poach an additional 5 minutes. Remove from heat. Spoon sauce from corners of pan over snapper until well blended with tomato sauce.

Yield: 4 servings

	RCU	FU	Cal	%Fat	P	F	C	Na
per serving	0	0	149	8	24	1	10	468

Fresh Spinach Salad with Apple-Nut Dressing

4	C	torn fresh spinach leaves
6		mushrooms, sliced
1		red apple, cored, sliced
1	C	Basic Dressing (*see recipe, Day 1, lunch*)
2	T	apple juice concentrate (unsweetened)
½	tsp	chicken bouillon granules
½	tsp	apple cider vinegar
2	T	Grapenuts cereal

Arrange fresh spinach leaves evenly on four salad plates. Top with mushroom slices. Place apple slices around the salad to form a border. In a small mixing bowl, whisk remaining ingredients together until blended. Ladle dressing evenly over salad. Serve.

Yield: 4 servings

	RCU	FU	Cal	%Fat	P	F	C	Na
per serving	0	0	136	11	12	2	20	324

Seasoned Noodles

1	lb	bag whole wheat noodles
1	pkg	Butter Buds
1	tsp	onion powder
1	tsp	garlic powder
½	tsp	black pepper

Prepare noodles according to package directions. After draining noodles, add Butter Buds and spices. Gently toss noodles to blend. Serve.

Yield: 4 servings

	RCU	FU	Cal	%Fat	P	F	C	Na
per serving	0	0	423	3	14	1	86	3

Fried Zucchini with Mushrooms and Onions

2		zucchini squash, sliced
4		mushrooms, sliced
1	sm	onion, cut julienne

Coat a saute pan lightly with a nonstick spray. Saute onions over medium heat until onions are transparent. Add zucchini and mushrooms; continue sauteing until vegetables are tender and golden brown.

Yield: 4 servings

	RCU	FU	Cal	%Fat	P	F	C	Na
per serving	0	0	31	6	2	T	7	5

Berries Melange Dessert

1	C	raspberries, fresh or frozen, unsweetened
½	C	boysenberries, fresh or frozen, unsweetened
½	C	strawberries, fresh or frozen, unsweetened
1½	T	apple-raspberry concentrate, unsweetened
½	C	plain nonfat yogurt
1	tsp	vanilla
1	tsp	cherry extract

Place strawberries, yogurt, concentrate, vanilla, and cherry extract in blender. Blend on high speed a few seconds. Refrigerate 1 hour before serving. Place raspberries and boysenberries in serving bowl. With a small spoon gently stir dressing; pour decoratively over berries. Garnish with strawberry roses.

Note: If you use fresh strawberries, wash and hull them.

Yield: 4 servings

	RCU	FU	Cal	%Fat	P	F	C	Na
per serving	0	0	59	5	2	T	12	24

For Strawberry Roses:

Place strawberry stem side down on countertop. Cut thin slices from the top to, but not through, the bottom of the strawberry. Spread the strawberry "petals" gently with your fingers.

Gifford's

DAY 7

BREAKFAST

PAGE 128

Assorted Fresh Fruit

"Country-Style Breakfast"

Scrambled Eggs

Seasoned Turkey Sausage

*Whole Wheat Buttermilk Biscuits
with Country Gravy*

LUNCH

PAGE 132

Stuffed Tomato with Chicken Salad

Assorted Fresh Vegetables

De-Lites Horseradish-Mustard Dressing

*Chilled Quartered Honeydew Melon
Topped with Sweet Nectar Dressing*

DINNER

PAGE 136

*The Gourmet Burger
with Sauteed Mushrooms and Lite American Cheese
on a Multi-Grain Bun*

Crisp Lettuce Leaf, Fresh Tomato Slices, and Sliced Red Onions

Baked Steak Fries

Gourmet De-Lites Ketchup

Creamy Refreshing Boysenberry Shake

Breakfast Menu Criteria

Products You'll Need

Scrambled Eggs:

Eggs

Sausage:

See recipe, Day 5, breakfast

Biscuits:

Whole wheat flour
Buttermilk powder (Saco brand)
Baking powder
Salt
Oil

Gravy:

Turkey sausage
Cornstarch
Onion powder
Chicken bouillon granules
Skim milk
Nonfat milk powder

**Assorted Fresh Fruit
   (your choice):**

Apples	Honeydew
Bananas	Nectarine
Cantaloupe	Oranges
Crenshaw	Peaches
Grapes	Pears
Grapefruit	Pineapple
Plums	

Helpful Menu Hints

1. If you already have frozen sausage patties on hand, simply remove them from the freezer and allow them to thaw in the refrigerator.

2. Prepare the gravy first, the biscuits second. Prepare the remaining menu items while the biscuits are baking.

3. For best results, serve the biscuits piping hot as soon as you remove them from the oven.

Food for Thought

Failures can be a foothold for success.

Breakfast Recipes

"Country-Style Breakfast"

Scrambled Eggs

2		eggs
4		egg whites, at room temperature
1	T	water

In a small mixing bowl, beat ingredients together until smooth and fluffy. Coat a skillet with a nonstick spray; pour the mixture into skillet and let the mixture begin to set over medium heat. Using a spatula, gently push mixture to center of skillet. Roll mixture only once, fluff gently.

Yield: 2 servings

	RCU	FU	Cal	%Fat	P	F	C	Na
per serving	0	1	111	45	13	6	1	169

Seasoned Turkey Sausage

See recipe, Day 5, breakfast.

Whole Wheat Buttermilk Biscuits

1	C	whole wheat flour
8	T	buttermilk powder (Saco brand)
2	tsp	baking powder
½	tsp	salt
1½	T	oil
¾	C	water

In mixing bowl, thoroughly stir together the flour, buttermilk powder, baking powder, and salt. Mix well to evenly distribute the baking powder and salt. Add oil and stir into mixture with a fork. Make a well in mixture; add water all at once. Stir just until dough clings together. On a lightly floured surface, knead dough gently 12 to 14 times. Roll dough to 1/2-inch thickness. Cut with a 2-inch biscuit cutter, dipping cutter in flour between cuts. Place biscuits on baking sheet. Bake in 425° oven for 10 to 12 minutes or until golden brown.

Yield: 12 biscuits

	RCU	FU	Cal	%Fat	P	F	C	Na
per biscuit	0	0	68	29	3	2	10	170

Country Gravy

2	oz	turkey sausage
½	C	water

Mix together:

1½	T	cornstarch
¼	C	water
1	T	onion powder
1½	tsp	chicken bouillon granules

Mix together:

1	C	skim milk
½	C	nonfat milk powder

In a small saucepan lightly coated with a nonstick spray, saute sausage until brown. Add water; stir. Bring mixture to a boil; add cornstarch mixture. Reduce heat to simmer. Stir well. Add onion powder and chicken bouillon granules. Stir. Add milk mixture slowly; blend well. Pour over biscuits and scrambled eggs if desired.

Yield: 4 (1/2 cup) servings

	RCU	FU	Cal	%Fat	P	F	C	Na
per serving	0	0	126	8	14	1	15	134

Lunch Menu Criteria

Products You'll Need

Chicken Salad:

Iceberg lettuce
Tomatoes
Chicken breast tenders
Celery
Basic Dressing (*see recipe, Day 1, lunch*)
Chicken bouillon granules
Onion powder
Celery seed
Cardamom
White pepper
Ground cloves
Apple juice concentrate (unsweetened)

Mustard Dressing:

Basic Dressing (*see recipe, Day 1, lunch*)
Dill pickle juice
Apple juice concentrate (unsweetened)
Prepared mustard
Prepared pure horseradish
Chicken bouillon granules
Onion powder
Celery seed
White pepper
Cinnamon

Nectar Dressing:

Honeydew melon
Apricot nectar
Pineapple juice concentrate
    (unsweetened)
Paprika
Nutmeg
Plain nonfat yogurt

Helpful Menu Hints

1. Prepare dressings first; both need to chill for one hour before serving.

2. This chicken salad recipe can also be used for sandwiches.

3. Horseradish-Mustard Dressing makes a tangy sandwich spread and a deliciously different vegetable dip.

Food for Thought

Set realistic goals; your realistic weight will not necessarily be the weight you have dreamed of.

Lunch Recipes

Stuffed Tomato with Chicken Salad

4	C	chilled iceberg lettuce, chopped
4	lg	tomatoes
1	lb	chicken breast tenders, cooked, diced
½	C	celery, finely diced
½	C	Basic Dressing *(see recipe, Day 1, lunch)*
1	tsp	chicken bouillon granules
1	tsp	onion powder
½	tsp	celery seed, ground
⅛	tsp	cardamom

dash of white pepper
dash of ground cloves

1	T	apple juice concentrate (unsweetened)

Place 1 cup of salad evenly on each individual plate. Core tomatoes. With stem end up, cut each tomato into 6 wedges, cutting to, but not through, base of tomato. Spread wedges apart slightly. Place tomatoes on salad, in center of each plate. In a medium mixing bowl, blend the chicken, celery, Basic Dressing, spices, and apple juice concentrate. Fill each tomato with about 1/2 cup of the chicken salad. Place assorted fresh vegetables around tomato.

Yield: 4 servings

	RCU	FU	Cal	%Fat	P	F	C	Na
per serving	0	.5	248	11	35	3	22	249

De-Lites Horseradish-Mustard Dressing

1½	C	Basic Dressing *(see recipe, Day 1, lunch)*
2	tsp	dill pickle juice
2	tsp	apple juice concentrate (unsweetened)
1	T	prepared mustard
1	tsp	prepared pure horseradish
1	tsp	chicken bouillon granules
1	tsp	onion powder
¼	tsp	celery seed

dash of white pepper
dash of cinnamon

In a small mixing bowl, gently whisk all ingredients together until smooth. Wait a few minutes, then whisk again. Chill for 1 hour before serving.

Yield: 8 (1/4-cup) servings

	RCU	FU	Cal	%Fat	P	F	C	Na
per serving	0	0	39	16	5	1	3	151

Honeydew Melon with Nectar Dressing

1		honeydew melon
½	C	apricot nectar (unsweetened)
3	T	pineapple juice concentrate (unsweetened)
1	tsp	paprika

dash of nutmeg

½	C	plain nonfat yogurt

Quarter honeydew melon. In a small mixing bowl, gently whisk remaining ingredients together. Chill 1 hour. Section honeydew. Pour dressing over fruit.

Yield: 4 servings

	RCU	FU	Cal	%Fat	P	F	C	Na
per serving	0	0	174	3	4	T	43	56

Dinner Menu Criteria

Products You'll Need

Burger:

Ground turkey
Grapenut cereal crumbs
Liquid smoke
Worchestershire sauce
Beef bouillon granules
Onion powder
Thyme
White pepper
Multi-grain buns
Mushrooms
Lettuce leaves
Tomato
Red onion
Lite American cheese

Ketchup:

See recipe, Day 4, breakfast

Steak Fries:

Potatoes
Beef bouillon granules
Onion powder
Garlic powder
Thyme
Paprika
White pepper

Shake:

Boysenberries, frozen
Skim milk
Nonfat milk powder
Apple-raspberry concentrate
    (unsweetened)
Crushed ice

Helpful Menu Hints

1.   Burgers, a traditional favorite, can be grilled, broiled, or barbecued. For a change of pace, try serving burgers with the barbecue sauce found on Day 14's dinner.

2.   Leftover potatoes can be chopped and used for hashbrowns.

3.   For this menu, prepare the potatoes first; they need to cook the longest.

Food for Thought

To understand the first time, always makes it easier the second time around.

Dinner Recipes

The Gourmet Burger

1	lb	ground turkey
½	C	Grapenuts cereal, finely crushed
½	tsp	liquid smoke
2	tsp	Worchestershire sauce
1	T	beef bouillon granules
1	T	onion powder
½	tsp	thyme
¼	tsp	white pepper
4		multi-grain buns
4		mushrooms, sliced, sauteed
4		lettuce leaves
1		tomato, sliced
1	sm	red onion, thinly sliced
4		Lite American Cheese slices, optional

In a large mixing bowl, combine ground turkey, Grapenuts, liquid smoke, worchestershire sauce, and spices. Blend well. With a moist hand, form mixture into 4 4-ounce balls. Place each ball on dry surface. Press on ball and form a pattie. Lightly coat a baking sheet with a nonstick spray. Place patties on baking sheet. Bake at 400° for 10 minutes. Remove from oven. Place sauteed mushrooms and cheese on top of each burger. Return to oven and bake until cheese melts, about 2 minutes. Serve on bun with lettuce, tomato and onion.

Yield: 4 burgers

	RCU	FU	Cal	%Fat	P	F	C	Na
per burger	0	1	345	15	32	6	42	332

Baked Steak Fries

4	med	potatoes, scrubbed
1	tsp	beef bouillon granules
2	tsp	onion powder
1	tsp	garlic powder
½	tsp	thyme
½	tsp	paprika
dash of white pepper		

In blender, combine all spices. Blend on high speed a few seconds. Pour spice mixture into shaker. Cut each potato lengthwise into 4 slices. Turn slices to lay flat, and slice potatoes 1/2 inch in width. Spray a baking sheet lightly with a nonstick spray. Place potatoes evenly on sheet. Sprinkle spice mixture over fries to cover. Bake at 400° for 30 minutes or until potatoes are cooked through and golden brown.

Yield: 4 generous servings

	RCU	FU	Cal	%Fat	P	F	C	Na
per serving	0	0	29	3	1	T	6	5

Gourmet De-Lites Ketchup

See recipe, Day 4, breakfast.

Creamy Boysenberry Shake

16	oz	frozen boysenberries (unsweetened)
4	C	skim milk
2	C	nonfat milk powder
1	C	apple-raspberry concentrate (unsweetened)
2	C	crushed ice

In blender, combine 4 ounces frozen boysenberries, 1 cup skim milk, 1/2 cup nonfat milk powder, 1/4 cup apple-raspberry concentrate, and 1/2 cup crushed ice. Blend on high speed 30 seconds. Pour shake into tall glass goblet or shake glass. Repeat procedure 3 more times to yield a total of 4 shakes. While making remaining shakes, place already-prepared shakes in freezer. Serve immediately.

Yield: 4 shakes

	RCU	FU	Cal	%Fat	P	F	C	Na
per shake	0	0	475	3	32	2	86	466

Gifford's

D A Y   8

BREAKFAST

PAGE 144

Gifford's Gourmet Strawberry Crepes
with Mock Sour Cream

Grilled Lyon Potatoes

Chilled Pear Halves with Juice

LUNCH

PAGE 148

De-Licious Fifteen-Bean Soup

Hot Buttermilk Muffins
with Fruit Preserves

Chilled Waldorf Salad
served on Crisp Red Leaf Lettuce

DINNER

PAGE 153

Chicken Cordon Bleu
with a Delicate White Sauce

Brown Rice Pilaf
with Scallions and Diced Carrots

Fresh Steamed Asparagus

Chilled Iceberg Salad
with Fresh Cucumber Slices
and Sweet Red Peppers

De-Lites Lemon Dressing

Hot Peach Cobbler

Breakfast Menu Criteria

Products You'll Need

Crepes:

Eggs
Skim milk
Nonfat milk powder
Apple juice concentrate
   (unsweetened)
Pure vanilla extract
Whole wheat flour
Baking powder

Potatoes:

Potato
Mushrooms
Zucchini
Red onion
Mozzarella cheese, part skim
Onion powder
Garlic powder
Black pepper

Strawberry Filling:

Strawberries
Plain nonfat yogurt
Basic Dressing
(see recipe, Day 1, lunch)
Apple-raspberry concentrate
   (unsweetened)
Cherry flavor extract

Remaining Menu:

Pear halves (in own juice)

Helpful Menu Hints

1. The crepe recipe makes 14 to 16 crepes, so you can freeze some of them for future use.

2. To freeze crepes, stack them alternately with two sheets of waxed paper. Place the stack in a moisture- and vapor-proof bag, and seal. When the crepes are frozen solid, place the stack in a glass or plastic container.

3. To use frozen crepes, remove the number of crepes you'll need and reseal the bag. Let the crepes thaw at room temperature for about 1 hour before filling them.

Food for Thought

Don't try to force ideas on someone else: he or she will follow the good example you set.

Breakfast Recipes

Gifford's Gourmet Strawberry Crepes

2		eggs
6		egg whites (at room temperature)
½	C	skim milk
½	C	nonfat milk powder
2	T	apple juice concentrate (unsweetened)
1	tsp	pure vanilla extract
1¼	C	whole wheat flour
½	tsp	baking powder

In a medium mixing bowl, combine the eggs, egg whites, skim milk, non-fat milk powder, juice concentrate, and vanilla. Whisk the ingredients together until smooth and fluffy. In a separate bowl, combine the whole wheat flour and baking powder. Stir thoroughly. Pour flour mixture slowly into egg mixture, stirring constantly until mixture is well blended. Lightly coat a griddle or skillet with a nonstick spray. Place griddle or skillet over medium heat. When hot, ladle 1/4 cup of mixture onto cooking surface and spread mixture in a circle to form a thin crepe. Cook through on one side until golden brown. Lift from surface by running spatula around edge to loosen, running spatula underneath crepe, and inverting onto a towel. Repeat with remaining batter.

Yield: 14 to 16 crepes

	RCU	FU	Cal	%Fat	P	F	C	Na
per crepe	0	0	136	12	10	2	20	124

Strawberry Filling

1	pint	strawberries, washed, hulled, sliced
½	C	plain nonfat yogurt
2	T	Basic Dressing *(see recipe, Day 1, lunch)*
2½	T	apple-raspberry concentrate (unsweetened)
1	tsp	cherry flavor extract

In a medium bowl, combine 1/2 the sliced strawberries and yogurt. Gently fold mixture until blended. In a cup, stir together Basic Dressing, apple-raspberry concentrate, and cherry extract until blended. Fold this mixture gently into yogurt and strawberries. Place a crepe onto a dry surface. Place 1 tablespoon of reserved strawberries in center; distribute evenly. Spoon 2 ounces of yogurt filling over strawberries. Fold 1/3 of crepe over mixture and roll. Place crepe on serving dish. Repeat procedure until all crepes are filled. Garnish with a dollup of yogurt and a strawberry slice.

Yield: filling for 16 crepes or 8 (2 crepe) servings

	RCU	FU	Cal	%Fat	P	F	C	Na
per serving	0	0	31	6	1	T	6	21

Lyon Potatoes

1	lg	potato, scrubbed, diced
2	C	water
4		mushrooms, chopped
1	sm	zucchini, chopped
1	sm	red onion, peeled, chopped
4	oz	shredded mozzarella cheese, part skim
1	T	onion powder
1	tsp	garlic powder
1	tsp	black pepper

In a medium saucepan, combine water and diced potatoes. Bring to a boil; cook until potatoes are tender. Drain water. In a skillet coated lightly with a nonstick spray, saute potatoes, zucchini, mushrooms, red onions, and spices over medium heat, stirring occasionally. Saute mixture until vegetables are tender and golden. Sprinkle mozzarella cheese over potatoes just before serving.

Yield: 4 servings

	RCU	FU	Cal	%Fat	P	F	C	Na
per serving	0	.5	83	27	6	3	11	285

Lunch Menu Criteria

Products You'll Need

Soup:

Fifteen-Bean Mix (Hamm's)
Celery
Onion
Carrots
Potatoes
Turkey ham
Chicken bouillon granules
Beef bouillon granules
Onion powder
Garlic powder
Ground cloves
Ground fennel
White pepper
Bay leaf
Worchestershire sauce
Tomato sauce
Tabasco sauce
Fresh parsley
Cornstarch

Muffins:

See recipe, Day 4, dinner

Preserves:

See recipe, Day 3, breakfast

Waldorf Salad:

Red delicious apples
Banana
Raisins
Celery
Plain nonfat yogurt
Apple juice concentrate
   (unsweetened)
Ground cinnamon
Ground nutmeg
Ground allspice
Ground cloves
Banana extract
Butter flavor extract
Red leaf lettuce
Grapenuts cereal

Helpful Menu Hints

1. Remember to soak the beans the night before preparing the soup.

2. If you have difficulty finding Hamm's Fifteen-Bean Soup Mix, ask your grocer; many stores are happy to order products they don't usually carry if customers request them.

Food for Thought

To achieve a good result, make a good effort.

Lunch Recipes

De-Licious Fifteen-Bean Soup

1	lb	Hamm's Fifteen-Bean Soup Mix, dry
4	qt	water
1	C	celery, diced medium
1	C	onion, diced medium
1	C	carrots, diced medium
1	C	potatoes, diced medium
½	C	turkey ham, diced medium
1½	T	chicken bouillon granules
1½	T	beef bouillon granules
1	T	onion powder
1	tsp	garlic powder
½	tsp	ground cloves
½	tsp	ground fennel
¼	tsp	white pepper
1		bay leaf
1	T	Worchestershire sauce
2	C	tomato sauce
½	tsp	tabasco sauce
2	T	fresh chopped parsley

Mix together (if needed as thickener):

3	T	cornstarch
½	C	water

Discard seasoning packet that accompanies the beans. Wash beans thoroughly. Cover with cold water. Add 1/2 teaspoon baking soda; stir, and soak beans overnight. Drain. Add four quarts fresh water. Bring beans to a boil. Reduce heat to simmer. Simmer beans for 1 1/2 hours, stirring occasionally. In a large skillet coated lightly with a nonstick spray, combine vegetables and turkey ham. Saute over medium heat until vegetables are tender. Take 1 cup liquid off the top of beans, add liquid all at once to vegetables and turkey ham. Stir well. Transfer vegetables and turkey ham to beans. Add remaining ingredients. Blend well. Simmer an additional 30 minutes, stirring occasionally. Remove from heat. Serve.

Yield: 8 servings

	RCU	FU	Cal	%Fat	P	F	C	Na
per serving	0	0	120	12	8	2	22	638

Hot Buttermilk Muffins

See recipe, Day 4, dinner.

Berry-Fruit Preserves

See recipe, Day 3, breakfast.

Chilled Waldorf Salad

2	lg	red delicious apples, cored, diced
1	med	banana, peeled, sliced
½	C	raisins
1		celery stalk, sliced
1	C	plain nonfat yogurt
3	T	apple juice concentrate (unsweetened)
½	tsp	ground cinnamon
¼	tsp	ground nutmeg
¼	tsp	ground allspice
⅛	tsp	ground cloves
¼	tsp	banana extract
¼	tsp	butter flavor extract
8		red leaf lettuce leaves, chilled
2	T	Grapenuts cereal (garnish)

In a medium salad bowl, combine apples, banana, raisins, and celery. Gently toss until blended. In a separate mixing bowl, combine yogurt, juice concentrate, spices, and extracts. Gently whisk ingredients until blended. Fold yogurt mixture into salad. Line a salad plate with 1 red leaf lettuce leaf. Spoon salad onto lettuce leaf. Sprinkle Grapenuts on top to garnish.

Yield: 8 servings

	RCU	FU	Cal	%Fat	P	F	C	Na
per serving	0	0	110	4	3	T	26	44

Pictured: De-Licious Four-Layer Lasagna, p. 171; Assorted Green Salad with De-Lites Sweet Basil Dressing, p. 172; Steamed Fresh Broccoli Spears with Mock Cheddar Cheese Sauce, p. 173.

Dinner Menu Criteria

Products You'll Need

Cordon Bleu:

Chicken breasts
Turkey ham
Onion
Mushrooms
Apple juice concentrate (unsweetened)
Chicken bouillon granules
Onion powder
Garlic powder
Dry mustard
Orange peel (dry)
Lemon juice
Cornstarch
Nonfat milk powder
Skim milk
Bleu cheese (aged)

Cobbler:

Peaches, sliced (frozen)
Cornstarch
Pineapple juice concentrate (unsweetened)
Apple juice concentrate (unsweetened)
Lemon juice
Ground cinnamon
Whole wheat flour
Buttermilk powder
Baking powder
Salt
Oil

Rice Pilaf:

Brown rice
Carrots
Scallions

Dressing:

Plain nonfat yogurt
Pineapple juice concentrate
  (unsweetened)
Lemon juice
Lemon peel (Schilling)
White pepper

Salad:

Iceberg lettuce
Cucumber
Red pepper

Remaining Menu:

Fresh asparagus

Pictured: Chicken Ala King, p. 55; Wild Rice Pilaf, p. 55.

Helpful Menu Hints

1. This menu is perfect for those times when you need a really elegant meal.

2. Serve the salad first.

3. If desired, you can spoon some of the white sauce from the chicken across the steamed asparagus.

4. After using your cutting board for meats and poultry, remember to scrub it well with hot soapy water before using it for any other foods.

Food for Thought

Whatever is worth doing at all is worth doing well."

Dinner Recipes

Chicken Cordon Bleu with a Delicate White Sauce

4		skinned chicken breasts
2	C	water
4		thin slices turkey ham
½	C	onion, finely chopped
3		mushrooms, finely chopped
1	T	apple juice concentrate (unsweetened)
1	tsp	chicken bouillon granules
1	tsp	onion powder
½	tsp	garlic powder
¼	tsp	dry mustard
¼	tsp	orange peel (dry)
1	tsp	lemon juice

Mix together:

3	T	cornstarch
½	C	water

3	T	nonfat milk powder
¼	C	skim milk
1	tsp	aged bleu cheese

On cutting board, remove each chicken breast from bone. Set breasts aside. Place breast bones in a medium saucepan. Cover with 2 cups water. Over medium-high heat, simmer bones for 10 minutes. Remove bones from saucepan and allow to cool. Set broth aside. Remove any additional meat from bones. Discard bones. Finely chop the chicken meat. In a skillet coated lightly with a nonstick spray, combine the chopped meat, onions, and mushrooms. Saute mixture until onions are transparent. Pour broth all at once into skillet. Stir thoroughly. Allow mixture to simmer. Add juice concentrate, spices, orange peel, and lemon juice; stir. Add cornstarch mixture, stirring constantly until mixture thickens. Reduce heat to low. Combine nonfat milk powder, skim milk, and bleu cheese in blender. Mix 5 seconds. Add this mixture to sauce. Stir thoroughly. Place chicken breasts flat in a 9X9 baking pan. Lay turkey

ham slice over each breast. Pour sauce evenly over breasts. Cover and bake at 350°
for 40 minutes. Serve over rice, spooning sauce over both. Garnish with lemon twists
and parsley sprigs.

Yield: 4 servings

	RCU	FU	Cal	%Fat	P	F	C	Na
per serving	0	.5	216	11	29	3	18	302

Brown Rice Pilaf with Scallions

2¼	C	water
1	C	brown rice
¼	tsp	salt
½	C	carrots, finely diced
2	T	scallions, chopped

Bring water and salt to a rolling boil. Add rice, carrots, and scallions. Stir. Reduce
heat to low. Cover tightly and simmer 45 minutes without removing cover.

Yield: 4 servings

	RCU	FU	Cal	%Fat	P	F	C	Na
per serving	0	0	190	5	4	1	41	148

Fresh Steamed Asparagus

asparagus, desired amount
water
salt

Remove woody bases from asparagus stalks by breaking stalks instead of cutting them; the stalk will snap easily where the tender part begins.

Add a dash of salt to 1 inch of water in saucepan. Bring water to a boil. Add asparagus stalks to boiling water, standing the stalks upright in the pan. Cover and cook 12 minutes.

Serving size = 1/2 cup

	RCU	FU	Cal	%Fat	P	F	C	Na
per serving	0	0	23	11	2	T	4	4

Garden Salad with Cucumber slices and Sweet Red Peppers

1 medium head iceberg lettuce
cucumbers
red peppers

Remove outer leaves of iceberg lettuce head. Discard any wilted or discolored outer leaves. Hit stem end sharply on tabletop to loosen core. Twist and remove core. Place lettuce head bottom side up, under cold water, and rinse well. Invert lettuce head and let water drain thoroughly. Place in plastic bag; refrigerate a few hours to crisp.

Tear lettuce leaves into pieces and place in salad bowl. (Chopping lettuce with a knife bruises th leaves.)

Garnish with slices of cucumber and red peppers.

Yield: approximately 4 servings

	RCU	FU	Cal	%Fat	P	F	C	Na
per serving	0	0	7	13	.6	T	1	5

De-Lites Lemon Dressing

1	C	plain nonfat yogurt
1	T	pineapple juice concentrate (unsweetened)
1	T	lemon juice
1	T	lemon peel (Schilling)

dash of white pepper

In a small mixing bowl, gently whisk all ingredients together until blended.
Yield: 5 (1/4 cup) servings

	RCU	FU	Cal	%Fat	P	F	C	Na
per serving	0	0	33	2	3	T	6	35

Hot Peach Cobbler

2	C	sliced peaches, frozen
3	T	cornstarch
2	T	pineapple juice concentrate (unsweetened)
2	T	apple juice concentrate (unsweetened)
1	tsp	lemon juice
1/2	tsp	ground cinnamon
1/2	C	whole wheat flour
4	T	buttermilk powder
1	tsp	baking powder
1/4	tsp	salt
2	tsp	oil
1/3	C	water

In small bowl, combine pineapple juice concentrate, apple juice concentrate, cornstarch, and lemon juice. Whisk until blended. In medium saucepan, combine peaches, cinnamon, and juice-cornstarch mixture. Cook over medium heat, stirring constantly until mixture thickens. Pour mixture into a 9x9 nonstick baking dish that has been lightly sprayed with nonstick coating. In separate mixing bowl, combine flour, buttermilk powder, baking powder, and salt. Stir thoroughly. Make a well in center of mixture. Pour oil and water all at once in well. Stir with a fork until mixture is moistened. Drop dough by the spoonful onto peach mixture. Bake in oven at 400° until cobbler is golden brown, about 20 to 25 minutes. Serve hot.

Yield: 4 servings

	RCU	FU	Cal	%Fat	P	F	C	Na
per serving	0	.5	191	15	5	3	37	258

Gifford's

D A Y 9

BREAKFAST

PAGE 164

Assorted Fresh Fruit

Cooked Whole Wheat Berries Topped with Blueberries

Sliced Bananas, Raisins

Skim Milk

English-Style Whole Wheat Muffin
with Preserves

LUNCH

PAGE 166

The California Fruit Salad

Hot Blueberry Muffins
with Fruit Preserves

DINNER

PAGE 169

De-Licious Four-Layer Lasagna

Assorted Green Salad

De-Lites Sweet Basil Dressing

Steamed Fresh Broccoli Spears
with Mock Cheddar Cheese Sauce

Strawberry-Banana Cream Pie

Breakfast Menu Criteria

Products You'll Need

Wheat Berries:

Whole wheat kernels
Blueberries, fresh or frozen
Banana
Raisins
Skim milk

Remaining Menu:

Whole wheat English muffins

Preserves:

See recipe, Day 3, breakfast

**Assorted Fresh Fruit
(your choice):**

Apples	Nectarine
Bananas	Oranges
Cantaloupe	Peaches
Crenshaw	Pears
Grapes	Pineapple
Grapefruit	Plums
Honeydew	

Helpful Menu Hints

1. Wheat berries can be served either hot or cold; for added flavor, stir in a small amount of your favorite unsweetened juice concentrate when serving.

2. Wheat berries can also be used as a crunchy salad topper--or even as a snack.

3. For variety, try using wheat berries as a substitute for rice!

Food for Thought

Do you know the ideal percentage of body fat for men and women? The range for men is 15 to 22 percent; for women, between 20 and 28 percent.

Breakfast Recipes

Cooked Whole Wheat Berries

1	C	whole wheat kernels
2	C	water
½	C	blueberries, fresh or frozen (unsweetened)
1		banana, sliced
2	T	raisins
1	C	skim milk

In a medium bowl, combine whole wheat kernels and water. Soak overnight; drain. Place soaked kernels in top of a double boiler with a small amount of water; pour 1 inch of water in the bottom of the double boiler. Cook kernels for 30 minutes over boiling water. Drain. Place half the amount of wheat berries in a bowl and stir in half the blueberries. Top with half the banana slices, raisins, and skim milk. Repeat for additional serving.

Yield: 2 servings

	RCU	FU	Cal	%Fat	P	F	C	Na
per serving	0	0	424	5	16	2	93	69

English-Style Whole Wheat Muffins

Purchase whole wheat English muffins; serve plain or toasted, as desired.

	RCU	FU	Cal	%Fat	P	F	C	Na
per muffin	0	0	135	7	5	1	26	364

Berry-Fruit Preserves

See recipe, Day 3, breakfast.

Lunch Menu Criteria

Products You'll Need

Salad:

Strawberries
Apple
Orange
Seedless grapes
Banana
Cantaloupe
Garden Salad
Low fat cottage cheese

Muffins:

See recipe, Day 1, lunch

Preserves:

See recipe, Day 3, breakfast

Dressing Supreme:

Raspberries, frozen
   (unsweetened)
Banana
Apple-raspberry concentrate
   (unsweetened)
Almond extract
Coconut extract

Helpful Menu Hints

1.   Any leftover fruit can be used later for fruit salad.

2.   Fruit with Fruit Dressing Supreme is also great as a dessert or a delicious snack!

3.   This menu, with its fresh fruits, is a real favorite during the summer months.

Food for Thought

It's nice to remind yourself that commitment, dedication, and desire are harvesting great rewards.

Lunch Recipes

The California Fruit Salad

1	C	strawberries, hulled, washed, halved
1	sm	apple, cored, quartered
1		orange, peeled, membrane removed, quartered
1	C	seedless grapes, rinsed
1	med	banana, cut into 1/2-inch slices
1		quarter cantaloupe, cut away from skin
2	C	chilled Garden Salad *(see recipe, Day 1, lunch)*
½	C	low fat cottage cheese

Arrange half the salad evenly on a large plate. Scoop 1/4 cup cottage cheese and place onto the center of the salad. Arrange half the fresh fruit around cottage cheese to edge of plate. Top with half the fruit dressing supreme. Repeat for second serving.

Yield: 2 servings

	RCU	FU	Cal	%Fat	P	F	C	Na
per serving	0	0	248	8	11	2	51	244

Hot Blueberry Muffins

See recipe, Day 1, lunch.

Berry-Fruit Preserves

See recipe, Day 3, breakfast.

Fruit Dressing Supreme

1	C	raspberries, frozen (unsweetened)
1	sm	ripe banana
2	T	apple-raspberry concentrate (unsweetened)
¼	tsp	almond extract
¼	tsp	coconut extract

Combine all ingredients in blender; blend on high speed for 30 seconds. Pour over fresh fruit on salad.

Yield: 5 (1/4 cup) servings

	RCU	FU	Cal	%Fat	P	F	C	Na
per serving	0	0	46	5	T	T	11	2

Dinner Menu Criteria

Products You'll Need

Lasagna:

Spaghetti Sauce
(see recipe, Day 2, dinner)
Whole wheat lasagna noodles
Low fat cottage cheese
Mozzarella cheese, part skim
Salt
Oil

Salad:

Head lettuce
Romaine lettuce
Endive lettuce

Dressing:

Basic Dressing *(see recipe, Day 1, lunch)*
Dill juice
Red wine vinegar
Lime juice
Apple juice concentrate (unsweetened)
Basil
Chicken bouillon granules
Garlic powder
Onion powder
White pepper
Cardamom

Broccoli:

Fresh Broccoli
Salt

Cream Pie:

Grapenuts cereal
Bananas
Apple-raspberry juice
   (unsweetened)
Banana extract
Cherry extract
Cornstarch
Fresh strawberries
Low fat cottage cheese
Apple juice concentrate
   (unsweetened)
Unflavored gelatin
Skim milk
Vanilla extract
Lemons

Cheddar Sauce:

Chicken bouillon granules
Onion powder
Butter Buds
Cornstarch
Skim milk
Nonfat milk powder
Yellow food coloring

Helpful Menu Hints

1. Make the pie a day ahead if you can; it needs to chill thoroughly.

2. Use care when freezing leftover lasagna; for best results, wrap individual serving sizes.

3. Be creative in using leftovers: you can combine leftover cheese sauce, cooked chopped broccoli, mushrooms, and diced pimiento for a delicious cheese and broccoli soup!

Food for Thought

Time management is simply the art of planning ahead.

Dinner Recipes

De-Licious Four-Layer Lasagna

1	qt	spaghetti sauce *(see recipe, Day 2, dinner)*
1	8-oz	box whole wheat lasagna noodles
1	pt	low fat cottage cheese, liquid drained
2	C	shredded mozzarella cheese, part skim
4	qt	water
½	tsp	salt
½	tsp	oil

In a large saucepan, bring water and salt to a boil; add oil. Add lasagna noodles one at a time, separating once with a spoon. Cook 10 to 12 minutes, or until done but not overcooked. Remove from heat. Drain, and rinse noodles under cold running water. Coat a 9x13x2 baking dish lightly with a nonstick spray. Put 1 layer of lasagna noodles in baking dish, overlapping each noodle. Spoon on enough sauce to lightly cover noodles. Repeat with cottage cheese; then sprinkle mozzarella cheese over cottage cheese. Repeat procedure until you have 4 layers, ending with sauce, cottage cheese, and mozzarella on top layer. Bake in oven at 350° for 40 to 45 minutes. Remove from oven. Let stand a few minutes before cutting to allow lasagna to settle. Cut lasagna into thirds lengthwise and into thirds widthwise.

Yield: 9 servings

	RCU	FU	Cal	%Fat	P	F	C	Na
per serving	0	2	308	32	27	11	25	617

Assorted Green Salad

1 medium head iceberg lettuce
1 medium head romaine lettuce
1 medium head endive lettuce

Remove outer leaves of iceberg lettuce head. Discard any wilted or discolored outer leaves. Hit stem end sharply on tabletop to loosen core. Twist and remove core. Place lettuce head bottom side up, under cold water, and rinse well. Invert lettuce head and let water drain thoroughly. Place in plastic bag; refrigerate a few hours to crisp.

For leaf lettuce, carefully wash and store each individual leaf in a plastic bag.

Tear lettuce leaves into pieces and place in salad bowl. (Chopping lettuce with a knife bruises the leaves.)

Yield: approximately 6 - 8 servings

	RCU	FU	Cal	%Fat	P	F	C	Na
per serving	0	0	7	13	.6	T	1	5

De-Lites Sweet Basil Dressing

1½	C	Basic Dressing *(see recipe, Day 1, lunch)*
1	tsp	dill juice
1	tsp	red wine vinegar
½	tsp	lime juice
1	tsp	apple juice concentrate (unsweetened)
1½	tsp	sweet basil
1	tsp	chicken bouillon granules
½	tsp	garlic powder
½	tsp	onion powder

dash of white pepper
dash of cardamon

In a small mixing bowl, gently whisk all ingredients until smooth. Chill. Gently whisk mixture again before serving.

Yield: 8 (1/4 cup) servings

	RCU	FU	Cal	%Fat	P	F	C	Na
per serving	0	0	37	15	5	1	3	127

Steamed Fresh Broccoli Spears

1	lb	fresh broccoli
		salt
		water

Wash broccoli and remove the outer leaves and tough parts of stalks. Cut broccoli lengthwise into uniform spears. Add salt to 1 1/2 inches water in saucepan. Bring to a boil. Add spears to boiling water. Cover and cook spears 10 minutes or until crisp-tender. Serve with mock cheddar cheese sauce.

Yield: 3 to 4 servings

	RCU	FU	Cal	%Fat	P	F	C	Na
per serving	0	0	12	11	1	0	2	144

Mock Cheddar Cheese Sauce

1½	C	water
1	tsp	chicken bouillon granules
1	tsp	onion powder
1	pkt	Butter Buds

Mix together:

1½	T	cornstarch
⅓	C	water

Mix together:

1	C	skim milk
½	C	nonfat milk powder

a few drops yellow food coloring

Combine water, chicken bouillon, onion powder, and Butter Buds in a small saucepan. Bring to a boil. Add cornstarch mixture slowly, stirring constantly until mixture thickens. Reduce heat to low. Add milk slowly. Stir. Add yellow food coloring. Ladle over steamed broccoli spears.

Yield: 8 (1/4 cup) servings

	RCU	FU	Cal	%Fat	P	F	C	Na
per serving	0	0	44	2	4	0	7	56

Strawberry-Banana Cream Pie

2	C	Grapenuts cereal, finely crushed
2	med	ripe bananas
2	C	apple-raspberry juice (unsweetened)
1	tsp	banana extract
1	tsp	cherry extract
5	T	cornstarch
1	C	strawberries, washed, hulled, sliced
1½	C	low fat cottage cheese
¼	C	apple juice concentrate (unsweetened)

Mix together:

1	T	unflavored gelatin
3	T	skim milk

½	tsp	pure vanilla extract

juice of 2 lemons

Coat a 10-inch glass pie plate lightly with a nonstick spray. Spread Grapenuts crumbs evenly over surface and press lightly with hand. Combine bananas, apple-raspberry juice, extracts, and cornstarch in blender. Blend on high speed 30 seconds. Transfer mixture to a medium saucepan. Cook mixture over medium heat, stirring constantly until mixture thickens. Pour mixture evenly over crumbs in pie plate. Place sliced strawberries evenly over banana mixture to cover. Combine cottage cheese, juice concentrate, gelatin mixture, vanilla, and lemon juice in blender. Blend on high speed for one minute. Pour mixture over strawberries evenly to cover. Chill for at least 6 hours, overnight if possible, before serving.

Yield: 8 servings

	RCU	FU	Cal	%Fat	P	F	C	Na
per serving	0	0	339	4	11	2	73	394

Gifford's

DAY 10

BREAKFAST
PAGE 178

*Buttermilk Pancakes
with Maple Syrup*

Chilled Grapefruit Halves

Broiled Turkey Ham Slices

LUNCH
PAGE 180

Chicken and Scalloped Potatoes

Crisp Celery and Carrot Sticks

*Strawberry Gelatin Whip Salad
served over Chilled Shredded Lettuce,
garnished with a Piece of Fresh Fruit*

DINNER
PAGE 184

Enchiladas Supreme

Spanish-Style Rice

Refried Beans

De-Licious Gaspacho Soup

De-Lites Mild Salsa

Key Lime Cheesecake

Breakfast Menu Criteria

Products You'll Need

Pancakes:

Whole wheat flour
Buttermilk powder (Saco brand)
Baking powder
Baking soda
Salt
Eggs
Apple juice concentrate (unsweetened)
Oil

Syrup:

See recipe, Day 2, breakfast

Remaining Menu:

Grapefruit
Turkey ham

Helpful Menu Hints

1.   For blueberry buttermilk pancakes, simply fold unsweetened blueberries (fresh or frozen) into pancake batter just before cooking.

2.   Substitute rye flour for wheat flour for a different but tasty pancake.

3.   Leftover pancake batter can be used for buttermilk muffins.

Food for Thought

Cantaloupe contains more B-vitamins and minerals than any other fruit.

Breakfast Recipes

Buttermilk Pancakes

1½	C	whole wheat flour
8	T	buttermilk powder (Saco brand)
1½	tsp	baking powder
½	tsp	baking soda
¼	tsp	salt
2		egg whites
2	tsp	apple juice concentrate (unsweetened)
2	tsp	oil
1¼	C	water

In a medium mixing bowl, combine flour, buttermilk powder, baking powder, baking soda, and salt; stir to mix well. Make a well in center of mixture. In a separate bowl, combine remaining ingredients. Beat until smooth and fluffy. Pour egg mixture all at once into well. Stir mixture just until moistened; mixture should still be lumpy. Pour 1/4 cup butter on a hot griddle or skillet for each pancake. Turn when pancakes are bubbly on surface or when golden brown.

Yield: 8 to 10 (4-inch) pancakes

	RCU	FU	Cal	%Fat	P	F	C	Na
per serving	0	.5	243	15	13	4	41	462

Maple Syrup

See recipe, Day 2, breakfast.

Lunch Menu Criteria

Products You'll Need

Chicken/Potatoes:

Boneless chicken breast tenders
Potatoes
Chicken bouillon granules
Onion
Celery
Onion powder
Dry mustard
Ground celery seed
White pepper
Cornstarch
Skim milk
Nonfat milk powder
Lite American cheese
Pimiento

Gelatin Whip Salad:

Unflavored gelatin
Apple-raspberry concentrate
  (unsweetened)
Cherry flavor extract
Crushed ice
Fresh strawberries
Plain nonfat yogurt
Shredded lettuce
Carrots
Celery

Helpful Menu Hints

1.   Serve chicken and scalloped potatoes in a casserole dish if you can.

2.   For variety, try raspberries, boysenberries, or blackberries in the gelatin whip salad.

3.   This menu can also be used for dinner.

Food for Thought

Do you know the five roadblocks to weight loss? They are food addictions, artificial sweeteners, food allergies, yeast overgrowth, and stress.

Lunch Recipes

Chicken and Scalloped Potatoes

1	lb	boneless chicken breast tenders
4	lg	potatoes, scrubbed, sliced 1/4 inch thick
4	C	water
1	T	chicken bouillon granules
1	lg	onion, cut julienne
2		celery stalks, cut julienne
2	T	onion powder
1	tsp	dry mustard
½	tsp	ground celery seed
¼	tsp	white pepper

Mix together:

3	T	cornstarch
½	C	water

Mix together:

1	C	skim milk
½	C	nonfat milk powder

4		slices, Lite American cheese
2	T	diced pimiento

Place sliced potatoes in a medium saucepan. Cover with 4 cups water. Bring to a boil; reduce heat and simmer potatoes until 2/3 done. Drain, reserving liquid. Set potatoes aside. In a skillet coated lightly with a nonstick spray, combine chicken tenders, onions, and celery. Saute until chicken is cooked through, stirring occasionally. Take 1 cup of reserved liquid and pour all at once over chicken and vegetables. Stir to gather caramelizing from pan. Pour juices from chicken and vegetables to pan with reserved liquid from potatoes. Bring to a boil. Reduce heat to simmer. Add chicken bouillon granules and spices; stir. Add cornstarch mixture slowly, stirring until mixture thickens. Add milk mixture slowly, stirring until blended. Remove from heat. Add cheese one slice at a time, folding cheese into sauce until cheese is melted. Add pimiento. Stir. Combine potatoes, chicken, onions, and celery in a 13x9x2 baking dish. Stir and spread evenly in dish. Pour cheese mixture over potatoes and chicken, folding gently until mixture is well blended. Bake in oven at 350° for 40 minutes.

Yield: 4 to 6 servings

	RCU	FU	Cal	%Fat	P	F	C	Na
per serving	0	1	359	12	44	5	33	825

Strawberry Gelatin Whip Salad

1	env	unflavored gelatin
1	C	apple-raspberry juice (unsweetened)
1	tsp	cherry flavor extract
1½	C	crushed ice
1	C	strawberries, washed, hulled, sliced
½	C	plain nonfat yogurt

Pour gelatin into mixing bowl. Combine apple-raspberry juice and extract in a small saucepan. Bring to a boil. Pour juice into mixing bowl with gelatin. Stir with a wire whip until gelatin is completely dissolved, about one minute. Add ice to mixture, whipping gently at first and then increasing the whipping speed as ice melts and gelatin starts to quick-set. Add strawberries. Stir. Add yogurt and fold into gelatin. Cover gelatin with plastic wrap. Chill for 1 1/2 hours. Scoop or spoon gelatin whip onto chilled shredded lettuce. Garnish with a piece of fresh fruit and carrot and celery sticks.

Yield: 4 servings

	RCU	FU	Cal	%Fat	P	F	C	Na
per serving	0	0	150	3	4	T	34	41

Dinner Menu Criteria

Products You'll Need

Enchilada:

Whole wheat flour tortillas
Boneless chicken breast tenders
Bell pepper
Onion
Diced green chilies
Chicken bouillon granules
Onion powder
Chili powder
Ground cumin
Garlic powder
Ground cloves
White pepper
Apple juice concentrate (unsweetened)
Tomato puree
Mozzarella cheese, part skim
Shredded lettuce

Salsa:

Tomato puree
Bell pepper
Onion
Apple juice concentrate (unsweetened)
Lemon juice
Lime juice
Chicken bouillon granules
Onion powder
Ground cumin
Chili powder
White pepper
Tabasco sauce

Spanish Rice:

Brown rice
Salt
Diced green chilies
Diced pimiento
Ground oregano
Onion powder

Beans:

Canned pinto beans
Apple juice concentrate
   (unsweetened)
Onion powder
Chicken bouillon powder

Gaspacho:

Tomatoes
Cucumber
Bell pepper
Celery
Onion
Tomato juice
Lemon juice
Apple juice concentrate
   (unsweetened)
Tabasco sauce
Chicken bouillon granules
Onion powder
Garlic powder
White pepper
Ground cloves

Pictured: Denver Omelet, p. 82; Gifford's Gourmet Strawberry Crepes, p. 146; De-Lites Mild Salsa, p. 189.

Products You'll Need (cont.)

Cheesecake:

Grapenuts cereal
Crushed pineapple
Low fat cottage cheese
Pineapple juice concentrate (unsweetened)
Apple juice concentrate (unsweetened)
Lime juice
Unflavored gelatin

Helpful Menu Hints

1. Make the cheesecake ahead of time.

2. Make the gaspacho first, then the salsa--both need to chill.

3. Leftover gaspacho can be ladled over vegetables, rice, and so on. The salsa is delicious on omelets and in Day 12's taco salad.

Pictured: Barbecued Chicken, p. 253; Potato Salad, p. 254; Creamy Fruit Salad Dessert, p. 256.

Food for Thought

The amount of saturated fat in vegetable and tropical oils ranges from 9 percent for safflower to 92 percent for coconut.

Dinner Recipes

Enchilada Supreme

4		whole wheat flour tortillas
8	oz	boneless chicken breast tenders
1		bell pepper, cut julienne
1	med	onion, cut julienne
1	T	diced green chilies
3	T	water
1	tsp	chicken bouillon granules
1	tsp	onion powder
¾	tsp	chili powder
¾	tsp	ground cumin
½	tsp	garlic powder
⅛	tsp	ground cloves
dash of white pepper		
2	tsp	apple juice concentrate (unsweetened)
1	C	tomato puree
2	oz	shredded mozzarella cheese, part skim
1	C	chilled shredded lettuce

In a large skillet, combine chicken breast tenders, bell pepper, and onion; saute over medium-high heat until tenders are cooked through and mixture is browned. Add green chilies and water all at once. Stir well to gather caramelizing from pan. Add remaining ingredients except mozzarella cheese and lettuce. Stir to blend well. Reduce heat to low. Cook on low 30 minutes, stirring occasionally. Let tortillas stand covered at room temperature a few minutes. Lay tortillas flat on a dry surface. Spoon equal amounts of filling into center of each tortilla. Sprinkle 1 ounce of mozzarella over filling. Fold 1/3 of tortilla to cover filling, then roll to finish. Place tortillas on a baking sheet coated lightly with a nonstick spray. Bake in oven at 350° for 12 minutes. Serve over shredded lettuce.

Yield: 4 servings

	RCU	FU	Cal	%Fat	P	F	C	Na
per serving	0	1	247	19	21	5	30	152

Spanish-Style Rice

1	C	brown rice
2¼	C	water
½	tsp	salt
2	tsp	diced green chilies
2	tsp	diced pimiento
½	tsp	ground oregano
½	tsp	onion powder

In a medium saucepan, bring water and salt to a boil. Add remaining ingredients; stir. Reduce heat to low; cover tightly and cook 50 minutes. Do not remove cover while cooking.

Yield: 4 servings

	RCU	FU	Cal	%Fat	P	F	C	Na
per serving	0	0	183	5	4	1	39	298

Note: Following are 2 options for refried beans. Notice the difference in %fat.

Refried Beans - Quick Method

1	15-oz can	pinto beans, without sugar
1	tsp	apple juice concentrate (unsweetened)
1	tsp	onion powder
½	tsp	chicken bouillon granules

Drain liquid from beans. In a colander, rinse beans under cold running water. Combine all ingredients in blender. Blend on medium speed until mixture is smooth. Transfer beans to a shallow saucepan coated lightly with a nonstick spray. Cook over medium heat, stirring occasionally for 10 minutes.

Yield: 4 servings

	RCU	FU	Cal	%Fat	P	F	C	Na
per serving	0	0	36	35	1	1	5	78

Refried Beans - Traditional Method

2	C	cooked pinto beans (1 cup dry pinto beans)
1	tsp	apple juice concentrate (unsweetened)
1	tsp	onion powder
½	tsp	chicken bouillon granules

Soak 1 cup beans overnight in 1 quart cold water. Drain. Add another quart of cold water over beans. Simmer for 1 1/2 hours, or till tender. Drain. Follow above cooking procedure starting at the blender.

Yield: 4 servings

	RCU	FU	Cal	%Fat	P	F	C	Na
per serving	0	0	28	12	2	T	5	55

De-Licious Gaspacho Soup

2	med	tomatoes, peeled, finely chopped
1		cucumber, finely chopped
1		green bell pepper, finely chopped
1		celery stalk, finely chopped
1	med	onion, finely chopped
2	C	tomato juice
2	T	lemon juice
2	T	apple juice concentrate (unsweetened)
½	tsp	tabasco sauce
1½	tsp	chicken bouillon granules
1	tsp	onion powder
½	tsp	garlic powder
dash of white pepper		
dash of ground cloves		

Combine all ingredients in a large jar. Cover tightly. Shake jar until well blended. Chill 2 hours before serving. Serve in soup cup. Garnish with a thin slice of lemon.

Yield: 4 servings

	RCU	FU	Cal	%Fat	P	F	C	Na
per serving	0	0	87	6	3	1	20	39

De-Lites Mild Salsa

1	C	tomato puree
1	sm	green bell pepper
1	sm	onion, peeled
1	T	apple juice concentrate (unsweetened)
1	tsp	lemon juice
1	tsp	lime juice
1	tsp	chicken bouillon granules
1	tsp	onion powder
½	tsp	ground cumin
¼	tsp	chili powder

dash of white pepper
5   drops tabasco sauce

Combine all ingredients in blender. Blend on high speed for 30 seconds. Chill.

Yield: 8 (1/4 cup) servings

	RCU	FU	Cal	%Fat	P	F	C	Na
per serving	0	0	24	6	1	T	6	9

Key Lime Cheesecake

2	C	Grapenuts cereal, finely crushed
½	C	crushed pineapple, with juice (unsweetened)
1½	C	low fat cottage cheese
3	T	pineapple juice concentrate (unsweetened)
3	T	apple juice concentrate (unsweetened)
½	C	lime juice
1	T	unflavored gelatin

Spray a 10-inch glass pie plate lightly with a nonstick spray. Spread crumbs evenly over surface and press lightly with hand. Place crushed pineapple in blender. Blend on whip until pineapple appears fluffy. Pour pineapple evenly over crumbs. Combine cottage cheese, juice concentrates, and lime juice in blender. Soften gelatin and dissolve in small amount of skim milk. Add dissolved gelatin to cottage cheese mixture. Blend on high speed until smooth. Pour evenly over pineapple and crumbs. Chill for 12 hours before serving.

Yield: 8 servings

	RCU	FU	Cal	%Fat	P	F	C	Na
per serving	0	0	180	5	10	1	34	373

Gifford's

DAY 11

BREAKFAST

PAGE 194

Assorted Fresh Fruit

Fresh Spinach and Mushroom Omelet

Golden Hashbrown Potatoes

Gourmet De-Lites Ketchup

*Whole-Grain Toast
with Preserves*

LUNCH

PAGE 197

Seafood Salad

*Hot Pineapple Muffins
with Almond Butter*

Fresh Fruit Garnish

DINNER

PAGE 202

*Beef Stroganoff
Served Over Wide Noodles
and Topped with Mock Sour Cream*

Steamed French-Style Beans

Lite Strawberry Parfait

Breakfast Menu Criteria

Products You'll Need

Omelet:

Fresh spinach leaves
Mushrooms
Omelet mixture
(see recipe, Day 4, breakfast)
Mozzarella cheese, part skim

For Preserves/Toast:

Whole-grain bread
Berries (unsweetened)
Apple-raspberry concentrate
(unsweetened)
Cornstarch

Hashbrowns:

See recipe, Day 4, breakfast

Ketchup:

See recipe, Day 4, breakfas

Assorted Fresh Fruit (your choice):

Apples	Nectarine
Bananas	Oranges
Cantaloupe	Peaches
Crenshaw	Pears
Grapes	Pineapple
Grapefruit	Plums
Honeydew	

Helpful Menu Hints

1. This menu provides an opportunity to use foods leftover from earlier menus.

2. Practice--you can prepare complete breakfast menus in half an hour or less.

3. If you can, use breakfast time to take inventory, go over upcoming meals, make shopping lists, and do other preparation.

Food for Thought

Don't be a victim of cynicism! Believe in and enjoy what you do!

Breakfast Recipes

Fresh Spinach and Mushroom Omelet

1	C	torn fresh spinach leaves
4	med	mushrooms, sliced
1	oz	shredded mozzarella cheese

Beat ometlet mixture until smooth and fluffy:

2	lg	eggs
4	lg	egg whites
½	tsp	chicken bouillon granules
2	T	water
pinch of pepper		

Combine spinach leaves and mushrooms in a small saucepan. Add just enough water to cover the spinach and mushrooms. Simmer until spinach leaves are wilted and mushrooms are tender. Drain. Coat an omelet or saute pan with a nonstick spray. Place over medium heat. When pan is hot, ladle 1/2 of the omelet mixture into pan; roll pan side to side until mixture covers pan. Reduce heat to low. Gently push one corner of egg mixture inward 1 inch and tilt pan toward you, enough to let remaining egg liquid roll out into pan to cover again. Add 1/2 amount of spinach and mushrooms to center of omelet. Sprinkle 1/2 of the mozzarella cheese on top. Fold 1/2 of omelet towards you to cover filling. Place spatula underneath omelet and fold over. Roll omelet out onto serving plate. Repeat procedure for second omelet.

Yield: 2 omelets

	RCU	FU	Cal	%Fat	P	F	C	Na
per serving	0	1	131	36	17	5	4	251

Assorted Fresh Fruit

(your choice)

Gourmet De-Lites Ketchup

See recipe, Day 4, breakfast.

Golden Hashbrown Potatoes

See recipe, Day 4, breakfast.

Berry-Fruit Preserves

1	C	berries, unsweetened, fresh or frozen
1	C	water
3	T	apple-raspberry concentrate (unsweetened)
2	T	cornstarch

Mix water and cornstarch together in a small saucepan. Over medium heat, stirring constantly, heat until mixture thickens. Remove from heat. Add concentrate; blend well. Add berries and gently fold into mixture.

Yield: approximately 1 pint or 16 (2 T) servings

	RCU	FU	Cal	%Fat	P	F	C	Na
per serving	0	0	13	2	T	T	3	1

Lunch Menu Criteria

Products You'll Need

Seafood Salad:

Iceberg lettuce
Tuna, canned
Chopped clams, canned
Cooked baby shrimp
Cooked crab
Basic Dressing *(see recipe, Day 1, lunch)*
Orange juice concentrate
(unsweetened)
Dill juice
Lemon juice
Chicken bouillon granules
Onion powder
Lemon peel
Dill weed
White pepper
Ground fennel seed
Assorted fresh vegetables
Lemon

Muffins:

Whole wheat flour
Bran, unprocessed
Baking powder
Baking soda
Salt
Egg whites
Oil
Skim milk
Pineapple juice concentrate
(unsweetened)
Crushed pineapple

Almond Butter:

Garbanzo beans (dry)
Cornstarch
Apple juice concentrate
(unsweetened)
Pure vanilla extract
Pure almond extract
Ground cinnamon

Helpful Menu Hints

1. This seafood salad also makes great sandwiches! The dressing for the seafood salad is also good by itself for garden salad or vegetable dip.

2. Save and freeze a few muffins for Day 14.

3. Almond butter is delicious stuffed in celery sticks or spread on toast or crackers.

Food for Thought

Webster's defines __starvation__ as to "perish or suffer from want of food." Dieting is not effective in controlling weight!

Lunch Recipes

Seafood Salad

2	C	iceberg lettuce, chopped
6½	oz	can tuna, packed in water, drained
6½	oz	can chopped clams, drained
4	oz	cooked baby shrimp
4	oz	cooked crab
½	C	Basic Dressing *(see recipe, Day 1, lunch)*
1	T	orange juice concentrate (unsweetened)
1	tsp	dill juice
1	tsp	lemon juice
1½	tsp	chicken bouillon granules
1	tsp	onion powder
1	tsp	lemon peel
½	tsp	dill weed

dash of white pepper
dash of ground fennel seed

In a medium bowl, combine tuna, clams, shrimp, and crab. Stir to blend well. In a separate bowl, combine remaining ingredients. Gently whisk until blended. Pour dressing over seafood. Fold dressing gently into seafood until blended. Arrange salad evenly on two salad plates. Scoop or spoon equal amounts of seafood salad onto salad. Garnish rest of salad with tomato wedges, lemon quarters, and assorted fresh vegetables if desired. Be creative!

Yield: 2 servings

	RCU	FU	Cal	%Fat	P	F	C	Na
per serving	0	1	360	12	62	5	14	1052

Hot Pineapple Muffins

1	C	whole wheat flour
1	C	unprocessed bran
1½	tsp	baking powder
½	tsp	baking soda
¼	tsp	salt
2		egg whites
2	tsp	oil
¾	C	skim milk
3	T	pineapple juice concentrate (unsweetened)
3	T	crushed pineapple, drained (unsweetened)

Lightly coat a nonstick muffin pan with a nonstick spray. In a small mixing bowl, beat egg whites with a fork. Stir in milk, juice concentrate, crushed pineapple, and oil. In a separate mixing bowl, stir together the flour, bran, baking powder, baking soda, and salt. Mix well. Make a well in the center of the mixture. Pour egg mixture all at once into well. Stir gently until blended. Spoon into prepared muffin pan, filling each cup 2/3 full. Bake in 400° oven 20 to 25 minutes. Serve hot or cold.

Yield: 12 muffins

	RCU	FU	Cal	%Fat	P	F	C	Na
per muffin	0	0	71	16	3	1	14	137

Almond Butter

4	C	garbanzo beans, dry
2	T	cornstarch
⅓	C	apple juice concentrate (unsweetened)
1	tsp	pure vanilla extract
1	tsp	pure almond extract
1	tsp	ground cinnamon

In a large saucepan, cook beans according to package directions. Drain, reserving 1 1/2 cups of liquid. On a nonstick baking sheet, arrange beans in a single layer. Bake at 350° for 1 1/4 hours, stirring often to toast beans evenly. Remove from oven and allow to cool. Transfer beans to blender; grind beans until smooth. In a medium saucepan, combine reserved liquid, starch, juice concentrate, vanilla, almond extract, and cinnamon. Whisk until mixture is blended well. Cook mixture over medium heat, stirring constantly until mixture thickens. Remove from heat. Stir ground beans into mixture. Blend well. Serve warm or chilled.

Yield: 32 (1 T) servings

	RCU	FU	Cal	%Fat	P	F	C	Na
per serving	0	0	41	13	2	1	7	5

Dinner Menu Criteria

Products You'll Need

Stroganoff:

Flank steak
Onion
Mushrooms
Apple juice concentrate (unsweetened)
Beef bouillon granules
Onion powder
Garlic powder
Basil
Paprika
White pepper
Worchestershire sauce
Kitchen Bouquet
Pimiento
Fresh parsley
Cornstarch
Whole wheat noodles
Salt
Plain nonfat yogurt

Strawberry Parfait:

Strawberries, fresh
Plain nonfat yogurt
Apple-raspberry concentrate
   (unsweetened)
Cherry flavor extract
Grapenuts cereal
Nonfat milk powder

Remaining Menu:

French-style green beans

Helpful Menu Hints

1. Prepare the parfait first; it needs to chill for two hours before serving.

2. Before you cut the flank steak, pound it on the countertop with a wooden mallet to tenderize it.

3. For a change of pace, serve stroganoff spooned over rice, or ladled over potatoes, or by itself.

Food for Thought

Good health is often a matter of good judgement.

Dinner Recipes

Beef Stroganoff

1	lb	flank steak, cut in strips
1	lg	onion, cut in 1-inch squares
6		mushrooms, quartered
3	T	apple juice concentrate (unsweetened)
¾	C	water
1½	T	beef bouillon granules
1	T	onion powder
2	tsp	garlic powder
1	tsp	basil
1	tsp	paprika
⅛	tsp	white pepper
1	T	Worchestershire sauce
1	tsp	Kitchen Bouquet
1	T	sliced pimiento
1	T	parsley, freshly chopped
1	C	water

Mix together:

3	T	cornstarch
½	C	water

In a large skillet lightly coated with a nonstick spray, combine flank strips and onion. Saute over high heat, stirring frequently, until browned. Add apple juice concentrate and water all at once. Stir well (to gather caramelizing from pan). Add beef granules, spices, Worchestershire sauce, and Kitchen Bouquet. Stir. Reduce heat to simmer. Add cornstarch mixture slowly, stirring constantly until mixture thickens. Add 1 cup water. Stir to blend. Simmer 30 minutes, stirring occasionally. Add mushrooms, sliced pimiento, and parsley. Stir. Simmer an additional 15 minutes, stirring occasionally. Serve over noodles, topped with a dollop of plain yogurt.

Yield: 4 (1 cup) servings

	RCU	FU	Cal	%Fat	P	F	C	Na
per serving	0	1	247	26	27	7	20	211

Wide Noodles

Cook wide whole wheat noodles according to package directions.

Serving size = 1 cup

	RCU	FU	Cal	%Fat	P	F	C	Na
per serving	0	0	200	11	7	2	37	3

French-Style Beans

Cook according to package directions.

Serving size = 1/2 cup

	RCU	FU	Cal	%Fat	P	F	C	Na
per serving	0	0	20	6	1	T	5	2

Lite Strawberry Parfait

1	C	fresh strawberries, sliced
1	C	plain nonfat yogurt
2	T	apple-raspberry juice concentrate (unsweetened)
1	tsp	cherry flavor extract
½	C	Grapenuts cereal, finely crushed
½	C	nonfat milk powder

Combine 1/2 the strawberries, 1/2 the yogurt, apple-raspberry concentrate, cherry extract, and nonfat milk powder in a blender. Blend on high speed until mixture is fluffy. Sprinkle small amount of Grapenuts crumbs on bottom of each of 4 tall parfait glasses. Spoon 1 ounce of remaining yogurt into each glass, pushing yogurt gently until level in glass. Spoon equal amounts of remaining strawberries into each glass to cover yogurt. Pour strawberry mixture evenly over strawberries. Garnish with remaining crumbs and a strawberry half. Chill 2 hours before serving.

Yield: 4 servings

	RCU	FU	Cal	%Fat	P	F	C	Na
per serving	0	0	162	2	11	T	30	225

DAY 12

BREAKFAST

PAGE 210

Chilled Strawberry Halves

Golden Belgium Waffles
served with Almond Butter

Strawberry Compote

Seasoned Turkey Sausage

LUNCH

PAGE 213

Taco Salad with Hot Salsa

Crisp Lettuce, Diced Tomatoes, Onions, and Bell Pepper
Topped with Mock Sour Cream

Spanish-Style Rice

Refried Beans

Chilled Cantaloupe Quarters

DINNER

PAGE 218

Breast of Chicken Florentine with Marinara Sauce

Brown Rice Pilaf

Three-Bean Salad on Red Leaf Lettuce
with Italian Dressing

Baked Yellow Squash with Nutmeg

Glazed Julienne Carrots

Desperado Dessert

Breakfast Menu Criteria

Products You'll Need

Waffles:

Whole wheat flour
Baking powder
Salt
Eggs
Skim milk
Oil

Sausage:

See recipe, Day 5, breakfast

Almond Butter:

See recipe, Day 11, lunch

Strawberry Compote:

Strawberries (unsweetened)
Apple-raspberry concentrate
    (unsweetened)
Cornstarch

Helpful Menu Hints

1. For added flavor, stir 2 packets of Butter Buds into the flour mixture while you are preparing the waffles.

2. For a future time-saver, make extra waffles now and freeze them.

3. For an on-the-go waffle sandwich, cut 1 waffle in half; spread it with almond butter, top with strawberry compote, and place the other half of waffle on top.

Food for Thought

Artificial sweeteners enhance the desire for sweets, cause many unpleasant side effects, and raise the fat thermostat. To find out more, read *The Bitter Truth About Artificial Sweeteners.*

Breakfast Recipes

Golden Belgium Waffles

1¾	C	whole wheat flour
1	T	baking powder
½	tsp	salt
1		egg yolk
3		egg whites
1¾	C	skim milk
1	T	oil

In a large mixing bowl, combine flour, baking powder, and salt. In a small mixing bowl, beat egg yolk with a fork. Beat in milk and oil. Add egg mixture to flour mixture all at once. Stir mixture until blended but still lumpy. Beat egg whites with electric mixer until stiff peaks form. Carefully fold egg whites into mixture. Leave a few fluffs of egg whites throughout the batter; do not overmix. Spray a waffle iron with a nonstick spray and preheat the waffle iron. When the iron is hot, pour batter onto waffle grids (check manufacturer's recommendations for amount of batter). Close lid quickly. Cook according to manufacturer's recommendations, or until waffles are golden brown. Remove cooked waffles with fork.

Yield: 4 waffles

	RCU	FU	Cal	%Fat	P	F	C	Na
per waffle	0	1	278	20	15	6	44	622

Almond Butter

See recipe, Day 11, lunch.

Strawberry Compote

2	C	water
1	C	frozen strawberries (unsweetened)
¼	C	apple-raspberry juice concentrate (unsweetened)

In separate bowl mix:

3	T	cornstarch
½	C	water

In a medium saucepan, bring water and juice concentrate to a boil. Slowly stir in cornstarch mixture. Reduce heat, stirring constantly until mixture is thick. Add strawberries and mix well. Remove from heat.

Yield: 6 (1/2 cup) servings

	RCU	FU	Cal	%Fat	P	F	C	Na
per serving	0	0	50	3	T	T	12	3

Seasoned Turkey Sausage

See recipe, Day 5, breakfast.

Lunch Menu Criteria

Products You'll Need

Taco Salad:

Corn tortillas
Ground turkey
Onions
Diced green chilies
Apple juice concentrate (unsweetened)
Chicken bouillon granules
Onion powder
Garlic powder
Chili powder
Ground cumin
Ground cloves
Tabasco sauce
Tomato puree
Shredded lettuce
Tomatoes
Bell peppers
Mozzarella cheese, part skim

Spanish Rice:

See recipe, Day 10, dinner

Refried Beans

See recipe, Day 10, dinner

Salsa:

Tomato puree
Bell pepper, green
Onion
Apple juice concentrate
  (unsweetened)
Lemon juice
Lime juice
Chicken bouillon granules
Onion powder
Ground cumin
Chili powder
White pepper
Tabasco sauce
Green chilies, diced
Cayenne pepper

Helpful Menu Hints

1. You can accompany this menu with any leftovers from Day 10's dinner.

2. Instead of rice and beans, serve gaspacho for a refreshing lunch. This menu can also be used as a dinner.

3. If you'd like to serve chips and salsa, simply cut corn tortillas into six pie-shaped wedges; spread out on a nonstick baking sheet, and bake at 375° until crisp.

Food for Thought

Here's another good reason to trim down: 80 percent of people with the type of diabetes that strikes in adulthood are overweight when they get the disease.

Lunch Recipes

Taco Salad

4		corn tortillas
8	oz	ground turkey
1	med	onion, finely chopped
1	T	diced green chilies
2	T	apple juice concentrate (unsweetened)
2	T	water
1½	tsp	chicken bouillon granules
1½	tsp	onion powder
1	tsp	garlic powder
1	tsp	chili powder
1	tsp	ground cumin
⅛	tsp	ground cloves
⅛	tsp	tabasco sauce
1	C	tomato puree
1	C	shredded lettuce, chilled
1	C	tomatoes, diced
1	C	green bell peppers, diced
1	C	onion, diced
2	oz	shredded mozzarella cheese, part skim

In a large skillet coated lightly with a nonstick spray, combine ground turkey and onion. Saute over medium heat until turkey is browned. Add diced green chilies. Stir. Add juice concentrate and water all at once to gather caramelizing from pan. Stir well. Add chicken granules and spices. Stir. Add tabasco and tomato puree. Blend well. Reduce heat to low; cover and cook mixture 15 minutes, stirring occasionally. Lay flat corn tortillas on a baking sheet. Bake at 375° for 12 to 15 minutes or until crisp. Remove from oven. Place tortillas onto 4 dinner plates. Spoon equal amounts of ground turkey mixture onto each tortilla; spread evenly to cover tortilla. Top each tortilla with equal amounts of the following in this order: shredded lettuce, diced tomatoes, green bell peppers, and diced onion. Sprinkle 1/2 ounce of shredded mozzarella cheese on each salad. Top with a hot or mild salsa. Garnish with a chilled cantaloupe quarter.

Yield: 4 servings

	RCU	FU	Cal	%Fat	P	F	C	Na
per serving	0	1	258	20	21	6	33	216

Spanish-Style Rice

See recipe, Day 10, dinner.

Refried Beans

See recipe, Day 10, dinner.

De-Lites Hot Salsa

1	C	tomato puree
1	sm	green bell pepper
1	sm	onion peeled
1	T	apple juice concentrate (unsweetened)
1	tsp	lemon juice
1	tsp	lime juice
1	tsp	chicken bouillion granules
1	tsp	onion powder
½	tsp	ground cumin
¼	tsp	chili powder

dash of white pepper
5 drops of tabasco sauce

| 1 | T | diced green chilies |
| ½ | tsp | red cayenne pepper |

Combine all ingredients in blender. Blend on high speed for 30 seconds. Chill.

Yield: 8 (1/4 cup) servings

	RCU	FU	Cal	%Fat	P	F	C	Na
per serving	0	0	24	6	1	T	6	9

Dinner Menu Criteria

Products You'll Need

Florentine:

Boneless chicken breasts
Spinach leaves
Mozzarella cheese, part skim
Onion
Celery leaves
Fresh garlic
Cooking sherry
Tomato puree
Chicken bouillon granules
Onion powder
Basil
Ground fennel seeds
Pepper
Fresh parsley

Squash:

Yellow squash
Butter Buds
Nutmeg

Glazed Carrots:

Carrots
Pineapple juice (unsweetened)
Orange juice (unsweetened)
Chicken bouillon granules
Cornstarch

Wild Rice Pilaf:

Wild Rice Pilaf mix

Salad:

Three-bean salad (canned)
Red leaf lettuce
Tomato
Red wine vinegar
Apple juice concentrate
   (unsweetened)
Chicken bouillon granules
Onion powder
Garlic powder
Oregano
White pepper

Dessert:

Frozen blackberries
Frozen boysenberries
Frozen raspberries
Frozen blueberries
Raisins
Grapenuts cereal
Plain nonfat yogurt
Apple-raspberry concentrate
   (unsweetened)
Black walnut extract
Cherry flavor extract
Coconut extract
Banana extract

Helpful Menu Hints

1.   This menu--one of my personal favorites--is featured in the cover photo. If you can, prepare it so it looks just like that picture, and you'll feel like a real gourmet!

Food for Thought

God grant me the serenity to accept the things I cannot change; courage to change the things I can; and wisdom to know the difference. (The Serenity Prayer.)

Dinner Recipes

Breast of Chicken Florentine with Marinara Sauce

4	5 oz	boneless chicken breasts
2	C	fresh spinach leaves, stems removed
4	1 oz	slices mozzarella cheese, part skim
1	C	water
1	sm	onion, finely chopped
¼	C	fresh celery leaves, finely chopped
3		cloves of garlic, pressed
1	oz	cooking sherry
1	29oz can	tomato puree
2	tsp	chicken bouillon granules
1	tsp	onion powder
1	tsp	basil
¼	tsp	ground fennel seeds
pepper to taste		
2	T	fresh chopped parsley

Cut chicken breast tenders from underside of chicken breast. Place chicken breasts and tenders in a baking dish. Pour in 1 cup water. Cover. Bake at 350° for 30 minutes. Remove from oven. Remove cover. Remove tenders and place on chopping board.

Drain stock from baking dish and reserve stock. Re-cover baking dish and place in oven on warm. Chop chicken tenders into fine pieces. In a large skillet lightly coated with a nonstick spray, combine chopped chicken tenders and onion. Saute over medium-high heat until onions are transparent, stirring occasionally. Add chopped celery leaves and garlic. Stir thoroughly. Add sherry all at once and move skillet briskly back and forth across burner. Add reserved stock all at once. Stir well. Reduce heat to low. Add tomato puree and spices; stir. Cook sauce on low for 15 minutes, stirring occasionally. Add chopped parsley just before serving.

Place spinach leaves in a medium saucepan with 1 inch of water. Cover pan. Steam until leaves are tender, about 2 minutes. Drain leaves, remove chicken from oven. Remove cover. Place equal amounts of spinach evenly on chicken breasts.

Place 1 slice mozzarella cheese for each breast to cover spinach. Place baking dish in oven at 300°. Bake just until cheese is melted.

Spoon brown rice onto 4 dinner plates. Spread rice out in the form of chicken breast. Ladle or spoon marinara sauce over rice. Place chicken florentine over rice. Ladle or spoon a small amount of sauce over center of florentine.

Yield: 4 servings

	RCU	FU	Cal	%Fat	P	F	C	Na
per serving	0	1	333	18	45	7	26	295

Wild Rice Pilaf

Prepare according to package directions.

Three-Bean Salad on Red Leaf Lettuce with Italian Dressing

15	oz can	three-bean salad mix
8		leaves red leaf lettuce
1	lg	tomato, sliced into 4 slices
1	tsp	red wine vinegar
1	tsp	apple juice concentrate (unsweetened)
½	tsp	chicken bouillon granules
½	tsp	onion powder
½	tsp	garlic powder
½	tsp	oregano

dash of white pepper

Drain liquid from the three-bean salad into a jar. Arrange 2 red leaf lettuce leaves onto each of 4 salad plates. Spoon equal amounts of three- bean mix onto each red leaf. Combine vinegar, juice concentrate, oil and spices with liquid in jar. Cover tightly. Shake dressing vigorously until blended well. Pour dressing over salads. Garnish each salad with a tomato slice.

Yield: 4 servings

	RCU	FU	Cal	%Fat	P	F	C	Na
per serving	0	0	46	12	4	1	9	13

Baked Yellow Squash with Nutmeg

1		approx. 8" by 4" piece yellow squash
1	pkt	Butter Buds
½	C	hot water
1	tsp	ground nutmeg
½	C	water

Cut squash into 8 2x2-inch squares. Using a fork, pierce 3 rows in each piece of squash. Stir Butter Buds into hot water. Spoon butter mixture evenly over squash. Sprinkle nutmeg evenly over squash. Place squash in a 9x9x2 baking dish. Pour in 1/2 cup water. Bake at 375° for 45 minutes or until squash is tender. Add more water to pan while baking if needed.

Yield: 4 servings

	RCU	FU	Cal	%Fat	P	F	C	Na
per serving	0	0	60	15	1	1	13	2

Glazed Julienne Carrots

2		carrots, cut julienne
3	C	water
3	T	pineapple juice (unsweetened)
3	T	orange juice (unsweetened)
1	tsp	chicken bouillon granules

Mix together:

3	T	cornstarch
½	C	water

In a medium saucepan, bring water to a boil. Add carrots. Reduce heat. Simmer until carrots are tender, about 10 minutes. Add juices and chicken granules. Stir. Add cornstarch mixture slowly, stirring gently until liquid thickens. Remove from heat. Serve with a slotted spoon.

Yield: 4 servings

	RCU	FU	Cal	%Fat	P	F	C	Na
per serving	0	0	91	2	1	T	22	21

Desperado Dessert

½	C	frozen blackberries
½	C	frozen boysenberries
½	C	frozen raspberries
½	C	frozen blueberries
½	C	raisins
½	C	Grapenuts cereal
1	C	plain nonfat yogurt
¼	C	apple-raspberry concentrate (unsweetened)
½	tsp	black walnut extract
½	tsp	cherry flavor extract
½	tsp	coconut extract
½	tsp	banana extract

Combine all ingredients in a large mixing bowl. Fold mixture briskly until blended well, about 5 minutes. (Rotate your arm while folding mixture.) Scoop desperado into an ice cream dish and serve.

Yield: 4 servings

	RCU	FU	Cal	%Fat	P	F	C	Na
per serving	0	0	204	3	6	1	47	150

Gifford's

D A Y 1 3

BREAKFAST

PAGE 228

Chilled Quartered Honeydew Melon

Hot Cream of Wheat Cereal
Topped with Grapenuts and Raisins

Sliced Bananas

Skim Milk

Whole-Grain Toast
with Preserves

LUNCH

PAGE 230

Chicken and Seafood Gumbo

Creamy Cole Slaw Salad

Fresh Pineapple Quarters

Whole-Grain Crackers

DINNER

PAGE 234

Sweet Pepper Cod

Spinach and Mushroom Salad
with Vinegar Dressing

Baked Potato with Mock Sour Cream

Steamed Zucchini and Tomato

De-licious Applesauce Cake

Breakfast Menu Criteria

Products You'll Need

Cream of Wheat Cereal:

Cream of Wheat
Salt
Grapenuts cereal
Raisins
Bananas
Skim milk

Remain menu:

Honeydew Melon

Whole-grain Toast:

Whole grain bread

Preserves:

Berries (unsweetened)
Apple-raspberry concentrate
   (unsweetened)
Cornstarch

Helpful Menu Hints

1.   You'll love this menu: it's quick and easy!

2.   For variety, garnish your cereal with cinnamon and dry orange peel.

Food for Thought

If you eat enough total calories and nutrients, your weight will come down naturally and comfortably. Best of all, it will stay at that lower level permanently!

Breakfast Recipes

Hot Cream of Wheat Cereal

Prepare according to package directions.
Top with Grapenuts cereal, raisins, bananas and skim milk.

Serving size = 1 cup

	RCU	FU	Cal	%Fat	P	F	C	Na
per serving	0	0	234	2	6	.6	52	239

Berry-Fruit Preserves

1	C	berries, unsweetened, fresh or frozen
1	C	water
3	T	apple-raspberry concentrate (unsweetened)
2	T	cornstarch

Mix water and cornstarch together in a small saucepan. Over medium heat, stirring constantly, beat until mixture thickens. Remove from heat. Add concentrate; blend well. Add berries and gently fold into mixture.

Yield: approximately 1 pint or 16 (2 T) servings

	RCU	FU	Cal	%Fat	P	F	C	Na
per serving	0	0	13	2	T	T	3	1

Lunch Menu Criteria

Products You'll Need

Gumbo:

Boneless chicken breasts
Potatoes
Onion
Celery
Carrots
Bell peppers
Zucchini
Mushrooms
Tomato puree
Skim milk
Nonfat milk powder
Chicken bouillon granules
Onion powder
Lemon peel
Dill weed
Ground mace
Ground fennel seed
White pepper
Dry mustard
Celery seed
Apple juice concentrate (unsweetened)
Lemon juice
Lime juice
Tabasco sauce
Liquid smoke
Cooked crab meat
Scallops
Cooked baby shrimp
Chopped clams

Cole Slaw:

See recipe, Day 6, lunch

Serve with:
Pineapple, fresh
Whole-grain crackers

Helpful Menu Hints

1. Don't be overwhelmed by the list of ingredients for gumbo--it's easy to prepare!

2. To save time, always put water in the pan first.

3. This hearty meal can also be used as dinner.

Food for Thought

The average woman eats about 2,000 calories daily, while the average man eats about 3,000 calories daily. Of these calories, 40 to 50 percent come from fats.

Lunch Recipes

Chicken and Seafood Gumbo

1	lb	boneless chicken breasts, cut in 1/2-inch cubes
2	C	potatoes, cut in 1/2-inch cubes
1	C	onion, cut in 1/2-inch cubes
1	C	celery, cut in 1/2-inch cubes
1	C	carrots, cut in 1/2-inch cubes
1	C	bell peppers, cut in 1/2-inch cubes
1	C	zucchini, cut in 1/2-inch cubes
1	C	mushrooms, quartered
1	C	water
1	C	tomato puree

Mix together:

1	C	skim milk
1	C	nonfat milk powder
2	T	chicken bouillon granules
2	tsp	onion powder
2	tsp	lemon peel
1	tsp	dill weed
½	tsp	ground mace
½	tsp	ground fennel seed
¼	tsp	white pepper
¼	tsp	dry mustard
¼	tsp	celery seed
2	T	apple juice concentrate (unsweetened)
2	tsp	lemon juice
1	tsp	lime juice
½	tsp	tabasco sauce
4	drp	liquid smoke
¼	lb	cooked crab meat
¼	lb	scallops
¼	lb	cooked baby shrimp
1	5½ oz can	chopped clams

Combine all ingredients, except seafood, in a large saucepan. Blend well. Bring mixture to a boil; reduce heat to simmer. Simmer mixture until vegetables are tender, about 30 minutes. Add all seafood. Simmer an additional 10 minutes. Remove from heat and serve.

Yield: 8 servings

	RCU	FU	Cal	%Fat	P	F	C	Na
per serving	0	0	270	8	33	2	30	481

Creamy Cole Slaw Salad

See recipe, Day 6, lunch.

Dinner Menu Criteria

Products You'll Need

Cod:

Cod fillets
Onion
Green bell pepper
Sweet red pepper
Mushrooms
Pineapple juice concentrate (unsweetened)
Lemon juice
Chicken bouillon granules
Lemon peel (Schilling)
Onion powder
White pepper
Cornstarch
Skim milk
Nonfat milk powder

Cake:

Whole wheat flour
Bran, unprocessed
Buttermilk powder
Baking powder
Salt
Ground cinnamon
Ground allspice
Eggs
Oil
Skim milk
Applesauce (unsweetened)
Apple juice concentrate (unsweetened)
Raisins

Salad:

Fresh spinach
Mushrooms

Dressing:

Plain nonfat yogurt
Red wine vinegar
Apple juice concentrate
 (unsweetened)
Chicken bouillon granules
Onion powder
White pepper
Mint flakes
Bay leaf

Potatoes/Mock Sour Cream:

Potatoes
Low fat cottage cheese
Plain nonfat yogurt
Unflavored gelatin
Onion powder
Lemon juice

Vegetable:

Zucchini
Tomato

Helpful Menu Hints

1. Prepare dressing and sour cream first, since they need to chill for an hour before serving.

2. When baking potatoes, pierce each one with a fork before baking.

3. Make your plate attractive by garnishing it with lemon crowns and fresh dill leaf.

Food for Thought

A hamburger, French fries, and shake from a leading fast food operation contain a total of almost 1,200 calories; 45 percent of those calories are from fat.

Dinner Recipes

Sweet Pepper Cod

4	4oz	cod fillets
1	sm	onion, cut julienne
1		green bell pepper, cut julienne
1		sweet red pepper, cut julienne
4		mushrooms, sliced
2	C	water
2	T	pineapple juice concentrate (unsweetened)
1	T	lemon juice
2	tsp	chicken bouillon granules
1	tsp	lemon peel (Schilling)
1	tsp	onion powder

dash of white pepper

Mix together:

3	T	cornstarch
½	C	water

Mix together:

½	C	skim milk
½	C	nonfat milk powder

Place cod fillets in a baking dish; pour 2 cups water over the fish. Bake at 350° for 20 minutes. In a large skillet lightly coated with a nonstick spray, combine bell pepper, sweet red pepper, and onion. Saute over medium heat until onion is transparent. Remove fillets from oven. Drain liquid from baking dish into skillet. Add mushrooms and allow to simmer. Add pineapple concentrate, lemon juice, and spices. Blend well. Add cornstarch mixture slowly, stirring constantly until sauce thickens. Add milk mixture, stir. Simmer for 5 minutes. Add cod fillets to sauce. Spoon sauce over fillets and allow to heat through. Place 1 cod fillet on each dinner plate and spoon sauce over each fillet.

Yield: 4 servings

	RCU	FU	Cal	%Fat	P	F	C	Na
per serving	0	0	215	3	28	1	23	180

Spinach and Mushroom Salad

4   C   torn fresh spinach leaves
6   mushrooms, sliced

Arrange fresh spinach leaves evenly on four salad plates. Top with mushroom slices. Ladle vinegar dressing evenly over salad.

Yield: 6 (1/4 cup) servings

Vinegar Dressing

1   C   plain nonfat yogurt
¼   C   red wine vinegar
2   T   apple juice concentrate (unsweetened)
1   tsp   chicken bouillon granules
1   tsp   onion powder
dash of white pepper
dash of mint flakes
1   bay leaf

In a medium mixing bowl, combine all ingredients except bay leaf. Gently whisk together until smooth. Add bay leaf. Chill for 1 hour, removing bay leaf when serving.

Yield: 6 (1/4 cup) servings

	RCU	FU	Cal	%Fat	P	F	C	Na
per serving	0	0	34	3	2	T	6	31

Mock Sour Cream

½   C   low fat cottage cheese
¼   C   plain nonfat yogurt
1   tsp unflavored gelatin (dissolve in small amount of skim milk)
1   tsp onion powder
1   tsp lemon juice

Combine all ingredients in blender. Blend on high speed until smooth (about 15 seconds). Chill for 1 hour before serving. Serve over baked potato.

Yield: 16 (1 T) servings

	RCU	FU	Cal	%Fat	P	F	C	Na
per tablespoon	0	0	11	12	2	T	1	32

Steamed Zucchini and Tomato

1   zucchini, sliced
1   tomato, sliced, halved

Combine zucchini and tomato in a saucepan with 1/2 inch of water; cover. Steam vegetables until tender, about 8 minutes.

Yield: 4 servings

	RCU	FU	Cal	%Fat	P	F	C	Na
per serving	0	0	50	6	2	T	12	433

De-Licious Applesauce Cake

2	C	whole wheat flour
1	C	bran, unprocessed
3	T	buttermilk powder
2½	tsp	baking powder
½	tsp	salt
1	tsp	ground cinnamon
½	tsp	ground allspice
2		eggs
2	tsp	oil
½	C	skim milk
1	C	applesauce (unsweetened)
3	T	apple juice concentrate (unsweetened)
½	C	raisins

Preheat oven to 375°. Coat a 9x13x2 nonstick baking pan with a nonstick spray. In a medium mixing bowl, stir together the flour, bran, buttermilk powder, baking powder, salt, and spices. Make a well in center of mixture. In a separate bowl, beat eggs with a fork. Stir in the oil, skim milk, and juice concentrate until blended. Add egg mixture all at once to well of flour mixture. Stir until moistened. Add applesauce and raisins. Beat mixture 30 strokes, being sure to scrape all dry ingredients from sides of bowl. Pour mixture into baking dish. Bake 35 to 40 minutes, or until a toothpick inserted into center of cake comes out clean. Allow to cool before cutting.

Yield: 24 servings

	RCU	FU	Cal	%Fat	P	F	C	Na
per serving	0	0	73	16	3	1	14	94

Gifford's

D A Y 1 4

BREAKFAST

PAGE 244

Fresh Chilled Pineapple Chunks

*Scrambled Eggs and Sauteed Eggplant
Topped with Mozzarella Cheese*

Homestyle Potatoes

Gourmet De-Lites Ketchup

Pineapple Muffins with Preserves

LUNCH

PAGE 247

The De-Lites Burger

Baked Steak Fries

Gourmet De-Lites Ketchup

Crisp Celery and Carrot Sticks

Fresh Fruit

DINNER

PAGE 251

Barbecued Chicken

Potato Salad

Corn-on-the-Cob with Almond Butter

Hot Whole Wheat Muffins

Creamy Fruit Salad Dessert

Breakfast Menu Criteria

Products You'll Need

Eggs/Eggplant:

Eggs
Eggplant
Mozzarella cheese, part skim

Pineapple Muffins:

See recipe, Day 11, lunch

Preserves:

See recipe, Day 3, breakfast

Potatoes:

See recipe, Day 4, breakfast

Gourmet De-Lites Ketchup:

See recipe, Day 4, breakfast

Remaining menu:

Pineapple chunks

Helpful Menu Hints

1.   Use a variety of vegetables with scrambled eggs if desired.

2.   Make enough ketchup to use for today's lunch, too.

3.   If you have leftover baked potatoes, slice them for hashbrowns.

Food for Thought

Remember to eat in harmony with the hunger drives of your body.

Breakfast Recipes

Scrambled Eggs and Sauteed Eggplant

2		eggs
2		egg whites, at room temperature
1	T	water
½	C	eggplant, peeled, diced
1	oz	shredded mozzarella cheese, part skim

Lightly coat a skillet with a nonstick spray. Saute eggplant until tender. In a small mixing bowl, beat eggs, egg whites, and water until smooth and fluffy. Add egg mixture to eggplant in skillet. Let mixture begin to set. Using a spatula, gently push mixture to center of skillet. Roll mixture over once; gently fluff. Sprinkle cheese over top of eggs before serving.

Yield: 2 servings

	RCU	FU	Cal	%Fat	P	F	C	Na
per serving	0	0	89	22	14	2	3	219

Baked Homestyle Potatoes

See recipe, Day 4, breakfast.

Gourmet De-Lites Ketchup

See recipe, Day 4, breakfast.

Pineapple Muffins

See recipe, Day 11, lunch.

Preserves

See recipe, Day 3, breakfast.

Lunch Menu Criteria

Products You'll Need

Burger:

Ground chicken
Grapenut cereal crumbs
Liquid smoke
Worchestershire sauce
Apple juice concentrate (unsweetened)
Lemon juice
Chicken bouillon granules
Onion powder
Ground thyme
Multi-grain buns
Mozzarella cheese, part skim
Lettuce leaves
Tomato
Yellow onion

Remaining menu:

celery
carrots
choice of fruit

Lemon Sauce:

Mock Sour Cream
(see recipe, Day 13, dinner)
Chicken bouillon granules
Lemon peel
Pineapple juice concentrate
     (unsweetened)
Lemon juice

Baked Steak Fries:

See recipe, Day 7, dinner

Gourmet De-Lites Ketchup

See recipe, Day 4, breakfast

Helpful Menu Hints

1. Keep your hands moistened with water--it makes it easier to form burger patties.

2. Burgers are also delicious char-broiled or grilled. Baking burgers keeps them moist inside.

3. This burger mixture can also be used as meatloaf by mixing in chopped onions and an egg.

Food for Thought

Diet and exercise; are a good marriage

Lunch Recipes

The De-Lites Burger

1	lb	ground chicken
½	C	Grapenuts cereal, crumbed
½	tsp	liquid smoke
2	tsp	Worchestershire sauce
1	tsp	apple juice concentrate (unsweetened)
1	tsp	lemon juice
1	T	chicken bouillon granules
1	T	onion powder
¼	tsp	ground thyme
4		multi-grain buns
4		thin slices, mozzarella cheese, optional
4		lettuce leaves
1		tomato, sliced
1	sm	yellow onion, thinly sliced

In a large mixing bowl, combine chicken, Grapenuts crumbs, liquid smoke, Worchestershire sauce, juice concentrate, lemon juice, chicken granules, and spices. Blend well. With a moist hand, form 4 4-ounce balls of meat mixture. Place each ball on a dry surface. With a moist hand, form a patty from each ball. Lightly coat a baking sheet with a nonstick spray; lift patties with a spatula onto the baking sheet. Bake at 400° for 12 to 14 minutes or until done. Place 1 slice mozzarella on each burger just before removing from oven. Serve on multi-grain bun with lettuce, tomato, and onion. Top off burger with Lite Lemon Sauce.

Yield: 4 servings

	RCU	FU	Cal	%Fat	P	F	C	Na
per serving	0	1	340	16	31	6	41	424

Lite Lemon Sauce

½	C	Mock Sour Cream *(see recipe, Day 13, dinner)*
½	tsp	chicken bouillon granules
1	tsp	lemon peel
2	tsp	pineapple juice concentrate (unsweetened)
1	tsp	lemon juice

In a small mixing bowl, gently whisk all ingredients until smooth.

Yield: 4 (3 T) servings

	RCU	FU	Cal	%Fat	P	F	C	Na
per serving	0	0	22	12	2	T	3	63

Baked Steak Fries

See recipe, Day 7, dinner.

Gourmet De-Lites Ketchup

See recipe, Day 4, breakfast.

Dinner Menu Criteria

Products You'll Need

Chicken:

Chicken breasts
Chicken legs
Yellow onion
Crushed pineapple
Apple juice concentrate (unsweetened)
Worchestershire sauce
Liquid Smoke
Tomato puree
Onion powder
Garlic powder
Chicken bouillon granules
Beef bouillon granules
Dry mustard
Vinegar
Kitchen Bouquet
White pepper

For Fruit Salad

Apples
Cantaloupe
Oranges
Honeydew
Bananas
Grapes
Pineapple chunks
Raisins
Plain nonfat yogurt
Pineapple-orange-banana
juice concentrate (unsweetened)
Coconut extract
Almond extract
Nutmeg

Potato Salad:

Potatoes
Onion
Celery stalk
Basic Dressing
(see recipe, Day 1, lunch)
Prepared mustard
Nonfat milk powder
Worchestershire sauce
Pineapple juice concentrate
(unsweetened)
Dill juice
Apple cider vinegar
Chicken bouillon granules
Onion powder
Dill weed
Celery seed
Cardamom
White pepper

Muffins:

Whole wheat flour
Unprocessed bran
Baking power
Baking soda
Eggs
Oil
Skim milk
Apple juice concentrate
(unsweetened)

Almond Butter:

See recipe, Day 11, lunch

Helpful Menu Hints

1. For a quick barbecue sauce, combine ingredients in blender. Blend on medium speed until blended.

2. Use this barbecue sauce on gourmet burgers, De-Lite burgers, meatloaf, and other meat dishes.

3. For a delicious grilled treat, use barbecue sauce on fish!

Food for Thought

To your health and to your new weight control program, I wish you the best. Bon appetit!

Dinner Recipes

Barbecued Chicken

1	lb	chicken breasts, skin removed
1	lb	chicken legs, skin removed
1		yellow onion, finely chopped
½	C	crushed pineapple, with juice
¼	C	apple juice concentrate (unsweetened)
2	T	Worchestershire sauce
½	tsp	liquid smoke
2	C	tomato puree
1	T	onion powder
1½	tsp	garlic powder
1½	tsp	chicken bouillon granules
1	tsp	beef bouillon granules
½	tsp	dry mustard
2	tsp	vinegar
1	tsp	Kitchen Bouquet

dash of white pepper

Coat a saucepan lightly with a nonstick spray. Saute onion over medium heat until onions brown. Add pineapple with juice. Stir thoroughly. Add remaining ingredients. Stir thoroughly. Simmer sauce for 20 minutes, stirring occasionally. In a large baking dish sprayed lightly with a nonstick spray, arrange chicken breasts and legs evenly. Ladle sauce evenly over chicken. Bake at 375° for 1 hour; during last 10 minutes, turn oven setting to broil to make chicken crispy.

Yield: 6 servings

	RCU	FU	Cal	%Fat	P	F	C	Na
per serving	0	.5	256	13	35	4	20	187

Potato Salad

4	lg	potatoes, cut in half, then sliced
1	sm	onion, minced
1		celery stalk, minced
1	C	Basic Dressing *(see recipe, Day 1, lunch)*
2	tsp	prepared mustard
3	T	nonfat milk powder
3	T	water
1	T	Worchestershire sauce
1	T	pineapple juice concentrate (unsweetened)
2	T	dill juice
2	tsp	apple cider vinegar
1	T	chicken bouillon granules
1	T	onion powder
1	tsp	dill weed
½	tsp	celery seed
¼	tsp	cardamom
¼	tsp	white pepper

In a medium saucepan, combine potatoes and water to cover. Boil potatoes 12 minutes or until tender. Drain. Transfer potatoes to a large mixing bowl. Add onions and celery. Stir. In a medium mixing bowl, combine remaining ingredients. Using a wire whip, whisk ingredients briskly until smooth and fluffy, about 1 1/2 minutes. Pour dressing over potato mixture. Stir mixture until potato salad is blended well and creamy. Chill before serving.

Yield: 6 servings

	RCU	FU	Cal	%Fat	P	F	C	Na
per serving	0	0	151	5	9	1	28	185

Almond Butter

See recipe, Day 11, lunch.

Hot Whole Wheat Muffins

1¼	C	whole wheat flour
¾	C	bran, unprocessed
1½	tsp	baking powder
½	tsp	baking soda
¼	tsp	salt
2		egg whites
2	tsp	oil
¾	C	skim milk
3	T	apple juice concentrate (unsweetened)

Coat a nonstick muffin pan lightly with a nonstick spray. In small mixing bowl, beat egg with fork; beat in milk, juice concentrate, and oil. In large mixing bowl stir together the flour, bran, baking powder, soda, and salt. Make a well in the center of the flour mixture. Add the egg mixture all at once. Stir gently just until blended. Spoon into the prepared muffin pan, filling each cup 2/3 full. Bake in 400° oven 20 to 25 minutes.

Yield: 12 muffins

	RCU	FU	Cal	%Fat	P	F	C	Na
per muffin	0	0	77	15	4	1	15	137

Creamy Fruit Salad Dessert

1	C	diced apple
1	C	diced cantaloupe
1	C	diced orange
1	C	diced honeydew
1	C	sliced banana
1	C	seedless grapes
1	C	pineapple chunks, drained
1	C	raisins
1	C	plain nonfat yogurt
½	C	nonfat milk powder
¼	C	pineapple-orange-banana juice concentrate (unsweetened)
¼	tsp	coconut extract
¼	tsp	almond extract

dash of nutmeg

Combine all fruit in a large mixing bowl. Fold until blended. In a mixer, combine remaining ingredients. Whip on medium-high speed until mixture forms soft peaks, about 1 minute. Pour topping over fruit. Gently fold until blended. Do not overmix. Chill 1 hour before serving.

Yield: 6 servings

	RCU	FU	Cal	%Fat	P	F	C	Na
per serving	0	0	265	3	8	1	62	93

Substitute Recipes

Gif's Chili - *A favorite of Health Resort clients*

4	qts	water
2	C	red kidney beans, dry
1	lb	beef flank steak, diced into small pieces
1	lg	bell pepper, diced
1	lg	onion, diced
2		celery stalks, diced
2	clove	garlic, minced
1	29oz can	tomato puree
¼	C	apple juice concentrate (unsweetened)
3	T	beef bouillon granules
2	T	onion powder
1½	T	chili powder
1	T	ground cumin
2	tsp	garlic powder
2	tsp	ground oregano
2	tsp	orange peel (Schilling)
½	tsp	liquid smoke
½	tsp	tabasco sauce
¼	tsp	white pepper

Soak beans overnight in cold water. Drain. In a large stock pot add 4 quarts of water to beans, bring to a boil. Reduce heat to simmer, cook beans for 1 1/2 hours or until tender; continue to simmer. In a large skillet sprayed lightly with a non-stick spray, saute steak flank pieces over medium heat until brown. Add bell pepper, onion, celery and minced garlic to skillet. Increase heat to high, stirring constantly, cook mixture until vegetables appear tender. Add apple juice concentrate all at once, blend well together, carmelizing from skillet. Transfer beef and vegetable mixture to beans in stock pot and blend well. Increase heat to medium add remaining ingredients, stir thoroughly. Cook chili an additional 30 minutes stirring occasionally.

Yields: approx. 1 gallon of delicious chili or 8 hearty servings

	RCU	FU	Cal	%Fat	P	F	C	Na
per serving	0	1	324	13	26	5	49	103

Serve with menu on Day 1, dinner or Day 4, dinner or create your own menu with this recipe.

Baked Orange Chicken

1	lb	chicken breast tenders
1	C	water
1	sm	onion, diced
3	T	orange peel (Schilling)
2	T	chicken bouillon granules
1	tsp	onion powder
¼	tsp	ground cinnamon
1	C	orange juice (unsweetened)
¼	C	pineapple juice concentrate (unsweetened)
3	T	cornstarch mixed with 1/2 C water
3	T	Grapenuts

Place chicken breast tenders evenly in a 9x13x2 baking dish. Add 1 cup of water to pan. Place pan in oven; bake at 350° for 30 minutes. In a small saucepan coated lightly with a nonstick spray, saute onions until tender. Add orange peel, chicken bouillon granules, onion powder, and ground cinnamon, blend well. Combine orange juice and pineapple juice concentrate; all at once and blend well. Bring mixture to a boil, add cornstarch mixture slowly, stirring constantly. Reduce heat to low and allow mixture to thicken. Pour orange sauce evenly over chicken. Sprinkle Grapenuts over top. Return to oven and bake an additional 15 minutes.

Yield: 4 (4-ounce) servings

	RCU	FU	Cal	%Fat	P	F	C	Naa
per serving	0	0	236	6	28	2	26	117

Serve with menu on Day 2, lunch, Day 3, dinner, Day 4, dinner, Day 6, dinner, Day 8, dinner, or create your own menu with this recipe.

Chicken Cacciatore

4	5oz	boneless chicken breasts, skin removed
8		chicken legs, skin removed
1	C	water
1	med	onion, cut julienne
1	lg	bell pepper, cut julienne
6	lg	mushrooms, quartered
2	clove	garlic, minced
1	29oz. can	tomato puree
3	T	apple juice concentrate (unsweetened)
1	T	Worchestershire Sauce
1	T	chicken bouillon granules
1	T	onion powder
1½	tsp	sweet basil
½	tsp	ground thyme
½	tsp	garlic powder
¼	tsp	white pepper

Place chicken evenly in a large baking dish. Pour in one cup water. In a large skillet coated lightly with a nonstick spray, combine the bell peppers, onions, minced garlic, and mushrooms. Saute over medium heat until vegetables are tender; add remaining ingredients. Blend well. Continue cooking this mixture over medium heat for 15 minutes stirring occasionally. Remove from heat. Pour sauce evenly over chicken. Cover pan. Bake in over at 375° for one hour. Remove from oven, remove cover, and serve.

Yield: 4 servings

	RCU	FU	Cal	%Fat	P	F	C	Naa
per serving	0	1	432	13	61	6	33	279

Serve with menu on Day 2, dinner, Day 9, dinner, Day 13, dinner, or create your own menu with this recipe.

Stuffed Bell Peppers with Tangy Tomato Sauce

6	lg	bell peppers
12	oz	cooked boneless chicken breasts, skinned, diced fine
1	med	onion, diced fine
1	C	cooked brown rice
3	T	De-lites ketchup *(see recipe Day 4, breakfast)*
½	C	tomato puree
1	T	chicken bouillon granules
1	T	onion powder
1	tsp	garlic powder
1	tsp	dry mustard
½	tsp	ground fennel

dash of white pepper
3 drops of liquid smoke

Cut top off of each pepper; remove the seeds and membranes from each pepper. Blanch peppers in enough boiling water to cover, for 5 minutes. Drain. In a large mixing bowl, combine remaining ingredients; mix well. Cut each pepper in half lenghwise. Spoon chicken mixture into each half to fill. Place pepper halves in a large baking dish evenly. Pour water into pan just to cover a half inch from the bottom. Bake in oven at 350° for 40 minutes.

Tangy Tomato Sauce

1	C	tomato sauce
½	C	skim milk mixed with 3 T non-fat milk powder
1	T	chicken bouillon granules
1	tsp	sweet basil
1	tsp	onion powder
½	tsp	garlic powder
1	T	apple juice concentrate (unsweetened)
1	T	red wine vinegar

Combine all ingredients in a small saucepan. Cook sauce over medium heat 15 minutes stirring occasionally. Ladle sauce over stuffed peppers.

Yields: 6 servings

	RCU	FU	Cal	%Fat	P	F	C	Na
per serving	0	0	180	8	18	2	24	407

INDEX

*J*ntroducing the new Green Valley Health Resort featuring the noted "How to Lower Your Fat Thermostat" weight control program.

One- to four-week live-in programs in Utah's Palm Springs.

Dieting doesn't work and you know it. The less you eat, the more your body clings to its fat stores. The only program that teaches you to eat to lose weight is the "How to Lower Your Fat Thermostat" program developed by Dennis Remington, M.D., Garth Fisher, Ph.D., and Edward Parent, Ph.D.—pioneers in the science of weight control and co-authors of the nationwide best-selling book "How to Lower Your Fat Thermostat"

Now, for the first time, their program is available on a full-time, live-in basis at the luxurious Green Valley Health Resort in St. George, Utah.

Under the direction of the doctors and staff at Green Valley, you will learn how your fat thermostat controls your weight and how you can control it. Your stay will include a private room, three hearty meals a day, fitness testing, seminars by health professionals, fitness and exercise classes, and recreational activities.

Green Valley—the Palm Springs of Utah—is a luxurious resort adjacent to eight national parks and home of the Vic Braden Tennis College. After a week with us, we'll revolutionize your thinking about weight control—for life!

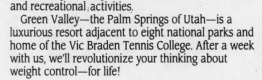

1515 W. CANYON VIEW DR.
ST. GEORGE, UTAH 84770

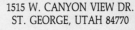

Toll Free 1-800-237-1068
In Utah Call (801) 628-8060

GREEN VALLEY HEALTH RESORT

How To Lower Your Fat Thermostat

Diets don't work and you know it! The less you eat, the more your body clings to its fat stores. There is only one program that teaches you to eat to lose weight and it's detailed here in this nationwide best-selling book. All other weight-control programs are based on caloric deprivation. The *How To Lower Your Fat Thermostat* program is based on giving you enough total calories and nutrients to convince the control centers in your brain that regulate fat stores that you don't need to hold onto that fat any more. Then your weight will come down naturally and comfortably, and stay at that lower level permanently.

Recipes To Lower Your Fat Thermostat

Companion cookbook to *How To Lower Your Fat Thermostat*. Once you understand the principles of the fat thermostat program, you will want to put them to work in your daily diet. Now you can with this full-color, beautifully illustrated cookbook. New ways to prepare more than 400 of your favorite recipes. Breakfast ideas. Soups and salads. Meats and vegetables. Wok food, potatoes, beans, and breads. Desserts and treats. All designed to please and satisfy while lowering your fat thermostat.

Acrylic Cookbook Holder

This acrylic cookbook holder is the perfect companion to your new cookbook. Designed to hold any cookbook open without breaking the binding, it allows you to read recipes without distortion while protecting pages from splashes and spills.

Five Roadblocks to Weight Loss (Audiocassette)

If you have a serious weight problem that has failed to respond to the fat thermostat program, then you could be suffering from any of the five roadblocks to weight loss: food addictions, artificial sweeteners, food allergies, yeast overgrowth, and stress. Learn what these roadblocks are, what to do about them, and how the fat thermostat program relates to them . . . in an exclusive interview with Drs. Dennis Remington and Edward Parent.

Pocket Progress Guide

A pocket-sized summary of the fat thermostat program that includes food composition tables, daily records, and a progress summary for quick and easy reference and record-keeping anytime, anywhere.

The Neuropsychology of Weight Control
(8 Audiocassettes and Study Guide)

Based on the best-selling book, *How To Lower Your Fat Thermostat*, this audiocassette program explains the principles of the fat thermostat program, then teaches you how to reprogram your fat thermostat for leanness. You will learn how to take control of your body and mind, how to determine your ideal body image, how to develop a fat-burning mechanism in the brain, and—best of all—how to develop a lifelong blueprint for leanness and health.

The Neuropsychology of Weight Control
(Videocassette)

For some people, seeing is believing. While reviewing the key points of the program and the benefits of reaching your goal weight, this motivational video also features testimonials by people who have had dramatic success. In moments of doubt or discouragement, this video provides the needed support and encouragement.

The Bitter Truth About Artificial Sweeteners

Research proves that those people using artificial sweeteners tend to gain more weight. Not only do artificial sweeteners enhance the desire for sweets, they also cause many unpleasant side effects in addition to raising the fat thermostat. Learn the real truth about artificial sweeteners and sugars. Learn how they affect your health and weight and what you can do about them.

The Neuropsychology of Weight Control
Personal Progress Journal

The journal will be your year-long record of how well you're doing. It also provides information on nutrition, exercise and health.

Back To Health: A Comprehensive Medical and Nutritional Yeast-Control Program

If you suffer from anxiety, depression, memory loss, heartburn or gas . . . if you crave sugar, chocolate or alcohol . . . if weight control is a constant battle . . . if you are tired, weak and sore all over . . . this book was written for you. While yeast occurs naturally in the body, when out of control it becomes the body's enemy, manifesting itself in dozens of symptoms. Getting yeast back under control can correct many conditions once considered chronic. More than 100 yeast-free recipes, plus special sections on weight control, hypoglycemia and PMS.

SyberVision's Neuropsychology of Self-Discipline
The Master Key to Success

There's one critical characteristic that makes the difference between success and failure; self-discipline. Without it, you can never hope to achieve your ambitions. With it, there's no goal you can't reach. *The Neuropsychology of Self-Discipline* is a unique self-improvement program that allows you to instill a new and powerful self-mastery into your own mind and body. Armed with tools, insights, and skills of a highly disciplined achiever, you'll be able, for the first time in your life, to systematically pursue and successfully realize your most important goals.

Desserts to Lower Your Fat Thermostat

If you think you have to say goodbye to desserts, think again.

At last there's a book that lets you have your cake and eat it too. *Desserts to Lower Your Fat Thermostat* is filled with what you thought you could never find: recipes for delicious desserts, snacks, and treats that are low in fat and free of sugar, salt, and artificial sweeteners.

The two hundred delectable ideas packed between the covers of this book meet the guidelines of both the American Heart Association and the American Diabetes Association. They will meet your own tough standards too — especially if you've been longing for winning ideas that will delight your family without destroying their health.

Gifford's Gourmet De-Lites

Vitality House is pleased to offer you an exciting work from a professional chef, Howard Gifford, whose meals have astonished guests lowering their fat thermostats at the Green Valley Health Resort. Says Howard, "I love to create that which is pleasing both to the eye and the palate. Preparing healthy food is my medium! My tools? The common everyday household kitchen conveniences found in most American homes today. 'Simplicity' is my watchword.

Become the creative gourmet cook you have always wanted to be! Learn what the magic of using just the right spices, extracts and natural juices can do for your foods! I'll also give you some helpful hints for shopping and organizing."

Qty.	Code	Description	Retail	Subtotal
	A	How To Lower Your Fat Thermostat	$9.95	
	B	Recipes To Lower Your Fat Thermostat	$14.95	
	C	Acrylic Cookbook Holder	$9.95	
	D	Neuropsychology of Weight Control ✳ (8 Audiocassettes and Study Guide)	$69.95	
	E	Back To Health	$9.95	
	G	Bitter Truth About Artificial Sweeteners	$9.95	
	H	Five Roadblocks to Weight Loss (Audiocassette)	$7.95	
	I	Pocket Progress Guide	$2.95	
	J	Neuropsychology of Weight Control (Videocassette)	$29.95	
	L	Neuropsychology of Self-Discipline ✳	$69.95	
	M	Personal Progress Journal	$14.95	
	N	Desserts to Lower Your Fat Thermostat	$12.95	
	O	Gifford's Gourmet De-Lites	$12.95	
	Z	Green Valley Health Resort Information Packet	FREE	
		Shipping and handling, $2.00 for the first item. (Within the United States)		$2.00
		Add an additional $.50 per item thereafter.		+
		Utah residents add 6.25% sales tax.		+
		Prices subject to change without notice.	TOTAL	

✳Purchase code "D" or code "L" and obtain your choice of a FREE book up to $14.95 in value. Be sure to indicate which book you would like!

☐ Check ☐ Money Order ☐ MasterCard ☐ VISA ☐ American Express

Card No. _____ Expires _____

Signature _____ Phone _____

Ship to: Name _____

Address _____

City/State/Zip _____

Mail to: Vitality House International, 1675 North Freedom Blvd. #11-C Provo, Utah 84604 (801) 373-5100

To Order: Call Toll Free 1-800-637-0708.